AN ILLUSTRATED HISTORY OF
AMPHIBIOUS
WARFARE VESSELS

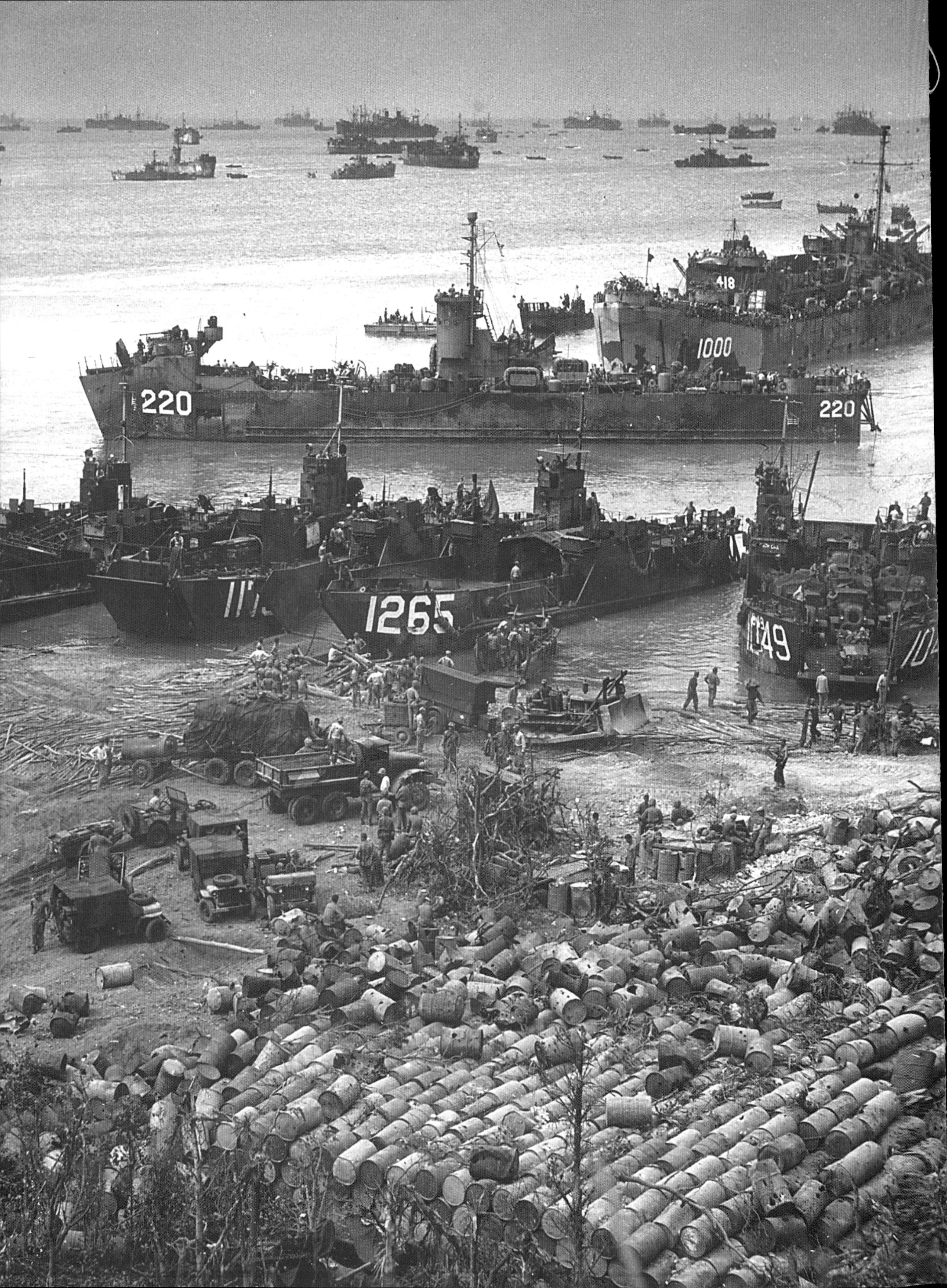
418
1000
220
220
1265
1049

AN ILLUSTRATED HISTORY OF
AMPHIBIOUS
WARFARE VESSELS

A COMPLETE GUIDE TO THE EVOLUTION AND DEVELOPMENT OF LANDING SHIPS
AND LANDING CRAFT, SHOWN IN 220 WARTIME AND MODERN PHOTOGRAPHS

BERNARD IRELAND

southwater

This edition is published by Southwater
an imprint of Anness Publishing Ltd
108 Great Russell Street
London WC1B 3NA
info@anness.com

www.southwaterbooks.com
www.annesspublishing.com

Anness Publishing has a new picture agency outlet for images for publishing, promotions
or advertising. Please visit our website www.practicalpictures.com for more information.

A CIP catalogue record for this book
is available from the British Library.

Publisher: Joanna Lorenz
Senior Editor: Felicity Forster
Production Manager: Steve Lang

Produced by JSS Publishing Ltd, Bournemouth BH1 4RT
Editor: Jasper Spencer-Smith
Designer: Nigel Pell
Indexer: William Jack

Previously published as part of a larger volume,
The World Encyclopedia of Amphibious Warfare Vessels

PUBLISHER'S NOTE
Although the information in this book is believed to be accurate and true at the
time of going to press, neither the authors nor the publisher can accept any legal
responsibility or liability for any errors or omissions that may have been made.

PAGE 1: **Operation "Overlord", Normandy.**
PAGE 2: **Operation "Iceberg", Okinawa.**
PAGE 3: **Two US Navy LCACs operating from a Wasp-class amphibious assault ship.**
PAGE 4 LEFT: **D-Day pre-landing operations, Weymouth, Dorset.**
PAGE 4 RIGHT: **USS *Blue Ridge* (LCC-19).**
PAGE 5 LEFT: **Operation "Avalanche", Salerno.**
PAGE 5 RIGHT: **Operation "Postern", New Guinea.**

Contents

Introduction   6

Categories of amphibious warfare   8
Gallipoli   10
Operation "ZO", Zeebrugge
   and Ostend   12
Plan Orange and a new rationale
   for the US Marine Corps   14
The Japanese Far East campaign   18
Operation "Jubilee", Dieppe   20
Operation "Watchtower",
   Guadalcanal   22
Operation "Torch", North Africa   24
Planning an amphibious operation   28
Command and Control (C2)   30
The amphibious force   32
Pre-landing operations   34
Securing the beachhead and
   breaking out   36
Logistics   38
Operation "Claymore",
   Lofoten Islands   40
Operation "Husky", Sicily   42
Operation "Avalanche", Salerno   46
The Pacific campaign   48

Operation "Toenails", New Georgia
   and Rendova   50
Operation "Postern", Lae/Salamaua,
   New Guinea   52
Operation "Galvanic", Makin
   and Tarawa, Gilbert Islands   54
Operation "Flintlock", Kwajalien,
   Marshall Islands   56
Operation "Overlord", Normandy   58
Operation "Infatuate II", Walcheren   64
Operation "Forager", Saipan,
   Marianas   66
New Guinea   68
Leyte Gulf   70
Operation "Detachment", Iwo Jima   72
Operation "Iceberg", Okinawa   76
DUKW   78
Operation "Chromite", Inchon, Korea   80
Operation "Musketeer", Suez   82
Operation "Starlite", Vietnam   84
Operation "Corporate", Falklands   86
The Middle East and current trends   90

Glossary   92
Index   94

Introduction

In the 14th century, small expeditions of determined men could achieve great things – Cortés and Pizarro waded ashore with battalion-sized forces and overthrew established civilizations in the name of gold and religion, resulting in the mainly Spanish-speaking subcontinent of South America. Since then, empires have been built and have collapsed, and colonies have been won and lost.

European colonial powers emerged, each with its own "sphere of influence". Each new colony developed fortified and garrisoned settlements and, as the new wealth was extracted, the hidden arm of seapower supplied the forces of administration and protection. Like tectonic plates, the spheres of influence tended to overlap to create great frictional forces along their boundaries. Great Britain, France, Spain and the Netherlands waged new-style wars, not on each other's sovereign territory but in lands far away. These, necessarily, were expeditionary wars and, as fortified settlements became better defended, so grew the requirement for the seaborne movement of military forces.

By more recent standards, however, numbers remained relatively small: Rooke's 2,000 marines sealed the fate of Gibraltar; Clive triumphed at Plassey with under 3,000 troops, while the disastrous capitulation of Cornwallis at Yorktown involved a force of only 7,000.

Ever-ambitious as a colonial power, Britain remained vulnerable to defeat by invasion. Unlike France, a rival and foe, Britain maintained no great standing army and the first, and effectively only, line of defence was the Royal Navy. This service also policed and protected a growing empire and trade routes; each ship on station was an amphibious force in miniature, able to field a self-contained "naval brigade" to calm any colonial uprising.

The South African ("Boer") War at the turn of the 20th century demanded considerable numbers of merchant ships, chartered to transport the horses upon which the mobility of the British Army depended. It really marked the end of the old-style colonial war, heralding a new era of alliances pitted against alliances, mechanization and modern weapons capable of inflicting death on a massive scale. With conflict in a worldwide arena, armies expanded, with constant movement not of thousands, but millions of troops.

A new front involved not only infantry but also transport and equipment. To rely on landing all this through established ports was to compromise the advantage of surprise.

The operations at Gallipoli thus showed the way forward with the landing over the beach of an initial one and a half divisions. The resulting casualties and variable pace of the operation demonstrated the need for, among much else, more specialist craft. Stalemate caused by a resolute defence resulted in valuable shipping being positioned offshore until enemy submarines arrived to make the situation untenable.

Between the wars Gallipoli was studied in detail, the lessons learned being tempered with the widely held opinion that the added dimension of air power might make such future operations impossible.

The 1930s nonetheless saw the development of the great assault fleet. Although operations were still envisaged on a relatively small scale, a clear requirement was apparent for two major categories of vessel, namely "ships" for shore-to-shore movement, possibly over considerable distances, and "craft" for ship-to-shore movement, the critical phase whereby the military component was landed.

The development complete, it needed only the requirements of World War II to initiate a combination of design ingenuity and industry to realize a large fleet, the likes of which the world had truly never seen.

This book details the development of amphibious forces through many theatres of combat. It highlights the activities necessary for a successful operation, from surveying and minesweeping to fire support, fighter direction and tri-service control. It includes analyses of naval operations in Gallipoli, Dieppe, the Pacific, Normandy, Leyte Gulf, Iwo Jima, Vietnam, the Falklands and the Middle East.

Amphibious warfare is again receiving considerable attention and investment by governments around the globe, and this book is, perhaps, a timely reminder of that fact.

RIGHT: **A vital element in amphibious operations in World War II was the pre-landing naval bombardment of enemy postions. Ships such as USS** *Tennessee* **(BB-43) would provide this massive firepower.**

ABOVE: **Japan successfully overran South-east Asia in 1942 with almost no specialist amphibious equipment, by boldly exploiting the unpreparedness and low morale of the poorly equipped defending forces.**

ABOVE: **The speed of the Landing Craft, Air Cushion (LCAC) permits, for the first time, Over-The-Horizon (OTH) operations, greatly reducing the vulnerability of valuable multi-purpose amphibious warfare ships.**

LEFT: **Marines and sailors from cutters landing at New Providence in the Bahamas on March 3, 1776. This was the first amphibious landing by American forces and was made to capture desperately needed munitions for use in the War of Independence, 1775–83. A force of 250 overran the British Fort Montague and later captured Fort Nassau along with 88 cannon, 15 mortars and a large amount of gunpowder.**

Categories of amphibious warfare

Current theory recognizes five categories of amphibious operation, namely assault, raids, demonstrations, feints and withdrawal. We naturally tend to think of these in the context of our own times, particularly of World War II, but the history of any traditional naval power will yield examples of how our forebears found solutions to relevant problems.

An assault is the primary form of operation, the objective of which is simply to establish a force on a hostile shore. This, in itself, has little point unless it is the precursor to occupation. This might well be the opening of a campaign but, although Normandy (1944) is easily remembered, Gallipoli (1915) or even the Norman Conquest (1066) are just as important.

An assault may have the alternative objective to seize a permanent base, from where more operations may be mounted. Numerous examples can be found during the war in the Pacific (1941–45); Gibraltar (1704) or Minorca (1708) were earlier examples of this type of operation.

A further assault objective may be occupation simply to deny a location to an enemy. During World War II the Azores, Iceland and Madagascar were all occupied, but an earlier parallel is seen in the British seizure of Trincomalee, Ceylon (Sri Lanka) from the Dutch in 1795. This was in order to deny the city and peninsula to the French, the new ally of the Dutch.

Raids are also an assault, but are of a size and configuration suited to a designated objective. There is also a time element involved, for once the objective has been achieved, the raiding force will need to be withdrawn. Local sea control, even if temporary, is thus a prerequisite. Raids, typically, are expensive in terms of casualties, as objectives tend to be well defended. Singular acts of personal courage also feature, but the chances of failure are relatively high. Modern successes include Pebble Island (Falklands, 1982) and St. Nazaire (1942); failures, Zeebrugge and Ostend (1918). Historically, Drake's brief occupation of Cadiz (1587), cost Spain dearly in materiel

RIGHT: **Royal Marines returning to Britain after the raid on Zeebrugge, April 1918. Of the 1,700 troops deployed, some 170 were killed and 300 injured. Eight of the raiding force were awarded the Victoria Cross. The operation was promoted as a British success by government propaganda.**

and treasure. Numerous later skirmishing expeditions were brilliant examples of small-scale raids, adding many useful prize ships to the strength of the Royal Navy.

A modern variation on the raid is to use sea and shoreline in manoeuvre warfare, undertaking "leapfrog" landings, known as "desants", to insert a small force in a strategically important location behind enemy lines until relieved by advancing friendly forces. This type of assault can be very destabilizing for an entrenched opponent; examples include those of the Soviet Union in the Black Sea, US and Australian forces in New Guinea and the British landing at Termoli on the Adriatic coast in 1943.

Demonstrations and feints are similar since both are calculated to confuse an opponent. A demonstration is staged with the objective of deceiving the opposition into shifting from a favourable to a less-favourable position, while a feint is designed to distract the enemy from the real danger. Because of the slow means of communication in earlier days, demonstrations and feints were applicable on a local level to military operations rather than to an amphibious assault.

Loading for an amphibious landing is a skilled and protracted operation and not practicable under fire. Large-scale withdrawals, therefore, tend to involve only personnel, with supplies and equipment being destroyed or abandoned. The withdrawals from Gallipoli (1915) and Dunkirk (1940) are modern examples, with others, such as Toulon (1793) and Corunna/Vigo (1809), featuring in history.

Withdrawal necessarily follows raids, with which heavy equipment is not usually associated. Most raids, such as those on Zeebrugge and St. Nazaire, require only what

RIGHT: **Armoured Amphibious Vehicles (AAV) of the US Marine Corps landing on Sattahip beach in eastern Thailand during exercise "Cobra Gold" on May 19, 2006. On the horizon is a US Navy Landing Ship, Dock (LSD).**

ABOVE: **Two Mulberry harbours were constructed, one at Omaha Beach (Mulberry "A") and the other at Arromanches (Mulberry "B") after the D-Day landings, June 6, 1944. Both were completed on June 9, but on June 19 a violent storm destroyed the harbour at Omaha. The remaining harbour at Arromanches (Port Winston) continued to be used for a further 10 months.**

might be termed man-portable equipment. An obvious and disastrous exception was the assault on Dieppe (1942). This operation suffered from problems that included the slow speed of Landing Craft, Tank (LCT), and the abandonment of all of the 29 Churchill tanks landed due to the shingle and the slope of the beach.

Gallipoli

The experience of Gallipoli was so awful that many were convinced that opposed landings were no longer feasible in the face of modern weaponry. As First Lord of the Admiralty, Winston S. Churchill conceived the notion of the Royal Navy forcing the Dardanelles, positioning off Constantinople (Istanbul) and threatening bombardment, forcing Turkey out of World War I.

With German advisers, however, the Turks had carefully mined the waterway, covering the minefields with shore-based artillery and searchlights. Following several attempts, resulting in both loss of life and ships, the Royal Navy had to admit defeat.

The adopted solution was to militarily seize the Gallipoli peninsula, which formed the northern side of the Dardanelles, thus allowing the fleet to pass. Gallipoli was suited to defence, being rugged, with parched hills cut by deep, dry gullies. The steep beach line offered few landing sites other than restricted coves, dominated by high ground.

ABOVE: **Naval and requisitioned commercial shipping was able to anchor off the Gallipoli beachhead only until the arrival of German U-boats.**

Commanding the Turkish forces was General Otto Liman von Sanders, a German officer who, to the Turks' natural bravery and fortitude, had imposed much-needed efficiency and discipline. Travelling the terrain thoroughly, he had identified and fortified all possible landing places. Barbed wire lined every beach, above and below water. Electrically controlled mines were buried in the beaches, all of which were covered by well-positioned machine-guns, providing enfilading fire over each cove from the high ground. Artillery, located further inland, was carefully directed on to intended target areas.

British planning was plagued by inter-service lack of contact, the Admiralty and War Office having differing aims. Personnel familiar with the terrain were not consulted, planning relying on out-of-date maps. To minimize casualties, the Army wanted a night landing; the Navy refused,

ABOVE: **HMS *Perdita*, a Royal Navy minelayer, leaving Mudros harbour to operate in the Dardanelles, 1916.** RIGHT: **With so much reliance placed upon ships' boats for troop movement, steam-powered picket boats from major warships were of crucial importance for towing lighters and other craft.**

citing inaccurate charts and possible mining. Preparations and stockpiling were lengthy and widespread, hopelessly compromising secrecy.

Around Cape Helles, at the tip of the peninsula, five beaches would be assaulted simultaneously by the British 29th Division. Fully equipped troops would be packed into open ships' boats, towed ashore in lines by steam pinnaces. At "V" beach only, the assault would be spearheaded by troops landing from *River Clyde*, a purposely modified Glasgow-built collier, which would be run ashore. Simultaneously, 32km/20 miles along the coast at Suvla Bay, the 3rd Australian Brigade would go ashore just before dawn to seize enemy positions and allow the landing of the 1st Australian Division and the New Zealand Brigade.

The operation was set for April 25, 1915. The ANZAC forces were landed at the wrong location, and hit by a determined Turkish counter-attack. Confined to a shallow beachhead the troops dug in and were not able to move forward.

At Helles, the *River Clyde* grounded too far out, her troops being cut down even as they struggled ashore. Troops packed in wooden boats were killed by machine-gun fire as the boats were impeded by underwater barbed wire. Beachheads were won, however, at all five locations, but at a dreadful price.

ABOVE LEFT: **Anzac Cove (Gaba Tepe) on the Gallipoli peninsula.** ABOVE: **HMT *River Clyde* ashore at "V" beach. Note the lack of damage, as all Turkish fire was of low calibre and mainly directed at moving troops and equipment.**

Great numbers of wounded died for lack of immediate surgical facilities, while medical evacuation was hopelessly inadequate. All areas were vulnerable to enemy fire, even the provision of water proving almost impossible. Naval support gunfire was available, but not effective against an enemy located in deep gullies. Heavy howitzers were required.

On the night of August 6/7, the British IX Corps was landed at Suvla to break the deadlock but leadership and motivation were poor. The situation remained static as before. This persisted, and disease began to claim as many lives as the Turkish bullets.

At home, there was a change of government and Churchill was removed from office. The Army commander, General Sir Ian Hamilton, was then replaced. Field Marshal Kitchener visited and, appalled by what he saw, decided to abandon the campaign which, in any case, had become rather irrelevant to the conduct of the overall war effort. During the night of January 8/9, 1916, some 17,000 men were evacuated by the Royal Navy in the only efficiently run part of the campaign.

LEFT: **Following the initial landings, most reinforcements could be brought ashore unopposed. Landing techniques had advanced little since the Napoleonic Wars.**

Operation "ZO", Zeebrugge and Ostend

The Belgian inland-waterway port of Bruges is connected to the sea, via canals, at Zeebrugge and Ostend. Occupied by Germany throughout World War I, Bruges was home to both destroyers and coastal submarines. Located so close on the flank of British shipping in the Strait of Dover, this presence was a continuous menace. In April 1918, the new Senior Naval Officer of Dover Command, Acting Vice-Admiral Sir Roger Keyes, revived a long-delayed plan to block both exits of the Bruges canal. Rather unimaginatively entitled "ZO", the operational plan was to use five small and obsolete cruisers as blockships, three at Zeebrugge, two at Ostend.

To this day, Zeebrugee lock entrance lays within the structure of the massive stone-built mole, which curves out to sea for over 1.6km/1 mile. On the outer side the mole forms a high, continuous wall; on the inner side it is a working quay. To permit water flow, the inshore 300 yards of the structure was built as an open, steel-framed viaduct.

Both ashore and on the mole extension were powerful batteries of guns. Those on the mole menaced the blockships at very close range, so Keyes proposed to neutralize them with a diversionary attack. An old submarine would first be expended to blow up the viaduct, preventing enemy reinforcement. Simultaneously, the old cruiser HMS *Vindictive*, modified for the occasion, would be lain alongside the outer wall, hard by the mole battery, which would be captured by a landing party. The blockships, meanwhile, would round the mole and be scuttled in the canal entrance. Their crews would be rescued by accompanying Motor Launches (ML).

The MLs would also lay a continuous chemical smoke screen. This was essential, though the night was moonless and it was high water. A first attempt at the raid, on the night of April 11/12, 1918, was abandoned due to a sudden shift in wind direction. In extricating the 70-odd craft from a point in mid-Channel, one small craft became detached. Running ashore, her papers were recovered by the enemy, thus compromising Keyes' plan. Ignoring this possibility, Keyes sailed again on the night of April 22/23.

In drizzling rain, HMS *Vindictive* emerged from the smoke screen rather short of the mole, just before midnight. Topside, awaiting orders to land, were 700 marines and 200 bluejackets. Swept by close-range fire, these suffered heavy casualties, including their leaders. Anxious to get alongside, the commanding officer of HMS *Vindictive* placed the ships 340 yards too far down the mole. The vessel was pinned in by a Mersey ferry, brought for the task, and the soldiers swarmed ashore over specially designed brows. Courage was never lacking, but human flesh was never a match for machine-guns and barbed wire. The gun battery on the mole was never taken.

ABOVE: **Acting Vice-Admiral Sir Roger Keyes with Earl Haig. In 1943, Keyes was created Baron Keyes of Zeebrugge and Dover.**

Just 55 minutes after landing, the assault party was recalled as the blockships arrived. The first, heavily hit by artillery at close range, staggered through a net boom and, her propellers fouled, she was scuttled clear of the entrance. The second, in contrast, was barely damaged and was carefully aligned for sinking, only to be hit by the third vessel. Both were then scuttled with explosives, the crews being safely taken off.

Aerial photographs taken the following day indicated that the latter pair of blockships had been well placed. Unfortunately, banks of silt had accumulated due to the

ABOVE: **The reason for the raid: a German submarine, based at Bruges, departing for a patrol against British shipping in the Channel or North Sea.**

ABOVE: **A navigable channel with a minimum low water depth of 4m/13ft existed to the right of the wrecks of HMS *Intrepid* (left) and HMS *Iphigenia*.**
RIGHT: **Motor Launches (ML) were used to lay a smoke screen to cover the attack, then to rescue the crews of the blockading vessels.**

neglect of the war years and the Germans experienced little difficulty in dredging a channel around the hulks, which, largely filled with concrete, were beyond easy salvage.

The Ostend part of "ZO" was a total failure. Shrewdly acting on information in the captured papers, the enemy simply moved navigation buoys. This elementary precaution was sufficient to see both blockships scuttled in entirely the wrong position. Three weeks later, the battered HMS *Vindictive* was expended in a second, but still only partially successful attempt, to blockade Ostend.

Operation "ZO" gave the British a moral boost but, with Bruges still working, was a failure. Eight of the force received the Victoria Cross; Keyes was knighted and 170 died.

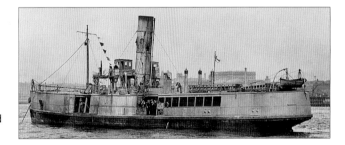

ABOVE: **HMS *Iris II*, one of the Mersey ferries at Liverpool docks after the raid. The other was HMS *Daffodil*.**
RIGHT: **An aerial photograph of the canal entrance after the raid. Note HMS *Thetis* at the entrance with HMS *Intrepid* and HMS *Iphigenia* across the waterway.**

Plan Orange and a new rationale for the US Marine Corps

In the early years of the 20th century, an accomplished small-boat sailor/gunrunner published a work of fiction that, myth has it, finally alerted the British establishment to the dangers inherent in burgeoning German naval power. Erskine Childers, author of "Riddle of the Sands", was something of a maverick and, having written the work by which he is remembered, came to a sad end, being executed during the Irish "troubles".

The parallels between Childers' progress and that of Lieutenant Colonel Earle H. Ellis, US Marine Corps, are interesting. Having written his prescient "Advanced Base Operations in Micronesia" in 1921 he applied for, and was granted, permission to travel incognito throughout the Japanese "Mandates" in an extraordinary role as a virtual freelance spy. Despite his service background, Ellis was also an intensely private individual who quickly "went native", marrying locally, and drank himself to an early death. First interred in Micronesia, his remains were exhumed and repatriated to the USA for burial. Because of official resistance to acknowledge the unorthodoxy of his odyssey, the truth emerged slowly and reluctantly, his fate becoming garlanded in myth and generally being attributed to the activities of the Japanese secret police. Nothing of further significance is believed to have resulted from his Micronesian wanderings, but his earlier book is widely credited as being a blueprint for the conduct of the Pacific War, 1941–45. This is, perhaps, a little facile, bearing in mind that US military plans for possible war with Japan had been initiated on the order of President Theodore Roosevelt.

ABOVE: **Plan Orange envisaged a trans-Pacific, island-hopping campaign, with Japan as the enemy. The US Marine Corps was virtually "re-invented" as the required assault force.** BELOW: **Boats now have engines but, over ten years after the Dardanelles disaster, landing techniques remain unimproved.**

LEFT: **Massed troops in unprotected wooden craft lacking ramps was not the ideal way to conduct an opposed landing. Fortunately, by August 1942 the US Navy had taken note and learned from British experience.**

Japanese–American relationships had deteriorated sharply in the first years of the 20th century. The Japanese annihilation of the Russian fleet at Tsushima (between Korea and Japan) in 1905 had been a sobering event, but also coincided with an unprecedented wave of Japanese emigration to the West Coast of the United States. At home, the US government was concerned at volatile interracial tensions; abroad it began to be worried at a newly confident Japan's expansionism. With the extensive Far Eastern interests of the United States under threat as he saw it, Roosevelt ordered military plans to be prepared against the possibility of hostilities. Thus began what would become Plan Orange, successively refined by generations of officers up until World War II.

The first full version of the plan appeared in 1911. The US Navy was then firmly Atlantic-centred. In those pre-Panama Canal days, it would take a full three months to get a battle-ready fleet to the Far East. The opening of the canal in 1914 shortened this somewhat. In the course of World War I, which was then commencing (and in which the United States remained uninvolved until April 1917), the US government learned that the British and Japanese, then bound by alliance, had agreed that German western Pacific island groups, notably the Marshalls and Carolines, would be mandated to the Japanese, while the southern groups would pass to the British. With the 1919 peace terms, these arrangements became official. Thus began the "Mandates question".

In 1921, the US government convened the Washington Conference, designed primarily to inhibit the ruinously expensive new naval arms race that had erupted between the late allied powers. In this it was successful in terms of capital

ships and also in obliging Great Britain to revoke the Anglo-Japanese alliance through agreeing to its dilution, about which the Japanese were unforgiving.

Article XIX of the ratified agreement expressly forbade further fortification, or the establishment of naval bases in detached Pacific territories which the major powers "may hold or hereafter acquire". This was something of a mixed blessing for the USA for, where Japan had no territorial interests in the eastern Pacific, the war with Spain in 1896 had made the United States a colonial power in the western Pacific.

ABOVE: **"Jacobs Ladders" were used widely during World War II to load follow-up troops into LCVPs alongside transports. With considerable sea motion, this was hazardous for heavily laden troops.**

15

Guam, in particular, was strategically significant, while the sprawling Philippines were more a social responsibility than an economic benefit. Neither could now be further fortified, nor could the United States afford to deploy a truly deterrent force. Owing to the proximity to Japan, early loss had, therefore, to be accepted in the event of war. This would leave the US government with two simple options – to accept the situation or to recover the territories. Of these, the first was not acceptable, leading inevitably to the second.

At this point the "Mandates" became significant, for any trans-Pacific expeditionary force would depend upon the US Navy for transport and support. During the late war the British had demonstrated the great potential of naval air power, and both the United States and Japan were working hard on naval aviation. The global aircraft carrier tonnage permitted to all

ABOVE: **In the background, even the relatively lightweight launches are shown grounded well away from the shoreline. Any fully equipped infantrymen stumbling and falling were in danger of being drowned.**

three was now bound by Articles VII to IX of the Washington Treaty but, in the myriad islands and atolls of the "Mandates", the Japanese had a deep natural barrier within which airfields could be constructed. Such land-based air cover would make US Navy fleet operations impossible. The "non-fortification" clause of the Treaty was, of course, expressly designed to prevent the creation of such facilities and, to their credit, the Japanese observed the prohibition. Unfortunately, they regarded the "Mandates" as a military area, and made foreign access difficult. With opportunities for inspection being impeded or forbidden, the US government assumed the worst.

LEFT: **The 30ft Eureka boat (in the foreground) could carry 18 troops, had a draft of 1.2m/4ft and no ramp. The "Artillery Lighter" in the next berth had a ramp at the stern.**

ABOVE: **An amphibious tank on trials at Culebra, Puerto Rico, in 1924. The vehicle was based on a Christie-type tank chassis.**

ABOVE: **US Marines practising leaving a troopship during an exercise at Quantico, VA, in the 1920s. The scrambling nets shown are of the same pattern as cargo nets used on commercial shipping.**

This, then, was the background to Ellis's "Advanced Base Operations in Micronesia". As the treaty allowed the United States to develop facilities only in Hawaii (Pearl Harbor) and on the West Coast, Ellis highlighted the requirement to develop the means and the techniques for seizing islands as "advanced bases", allowing a steady westward advance across the Pacific.

Marines had been used traditionally by all major fleets for landing duties. During World War I, marine forces of both the United States and Great Britain had been expanded to the point where marine brigades had served ashore alongside regular Army infantry. Over the years, the US Marine Corps (USMC) was used extensively to maintain peace in the Caribbean and in Central America. Post-war reductions and economies, however, had seen the USMC reduced to the point where its future seemed limited to small-scale policing, shipboard detachments, ceremonial and guarding fleet bases. There were even those who advocated disbandment.

Ellis now eloquently justified the creation of an "Advanced Base Force". With Japan in mind as the most likely future enemy and the British failure at Gallipoli as a template from which to learn, the USMC began a transition to a fully self-contained expeditionary force, constituted as elements of both the US Navy Atlantic and Pacific fleets. In 1933, the arrangement was formalized as the "Fleet Marine Force" (FMF), with a strength of two independent 1,600-man battalions. These would be in addition to smaller detachments for minor commitments. Their purpose was to train and to develop equipment for amphibious warfare.

The USMC had its own, dedicated transport, the USS *Henderson* (AP-1), built to specific requirements during World War I. Interestingly, for future categorization, AP-1 was designed to land troops as a fully contained combat unit, a distinction that saw the ship classed as an "expeditionary transport" (later AK "attack transport") as opposed to what were called by the British "troopships" and, by the US Navy, "convoy transport". Attack transports had to sacrifice some troop accommodation for extra equipment stowage.

Amphibious exercises, termed "Fleet Landing Exercises" (FLEX), were conducted regularly during the 1930s. Despite restricted budgets, accumulated experience resulted in the production of the "Tentative Landing Operations Manual" (TLOM), which, with updates, was adopted formally in 1938 as the US Navy's "Landing Operations Doctrine" (LOD). Many basic operational elements had, by now, been reasonably developed, including the value of a USMC aviation component for ground support, warship-based gunfire support, amphibious armour and the ramped small craft necessary for the delivery of artillery and vehicles over the beach. Boatbuilder Andrew Jackson Higgins had already begun his fruitful cooperation with the policy makers. By 1941, the FMF had a strength of some 23,000 men.

17

LEFT: **The Japanese occupation of Guam as seen by the artist Kohei Ezaki for a propoganda book. The preferred technique was to mount several simultaneous assaults over related, undefended beaches.**

The Japanese Far East campaign

By far the world's most experienced power in amphibious warfare, the Japanese had perfected their techniques in over ten years of war with China. National pride had been slighted at the 1921–22 Washington Conference, where the major powers had not accorded the Japanese the status of a first rank naval power. Relegated to quantitative inferiority, Japan's forces henceforth strove for qualitative superiority and, by December 1941, had achieved this aim.

A central belief of the ruling elite, political as well as military, was that the nation must, at some stage, extend its frontiers to provide both the space and natural resources required. The most attractive option was to capture the Dutch East Indies and Malaya (now Indonesia and Malaysia), risking war with the region's colonial powers – the United States, Britain, the Netherlands and France. By December 1941, however, the last two were already out of the war and Britain appeared weakened. The time was right.

Since 1923, when the USA was declared the most likely future enemy, the Japanese Army had concentrated on developing techniques and plans for regional conquest, while the Japanese Navy had prepared for a Trafalgar-style battle with the US Navy spearheading the inevitable counter-attack.

In general, the army and navy did not enjoy good relations, with a degree of harmony continuously existing only in amphibious warfare. Realistic exercises developed rules for naval gunfire support, ship-to-shore procedures, the need for specialist craft and for air superiority.

Unhappy early experience in China led the Japanese to favour unopposed landings by night. In contrast to later US forces "wave" assaults, these were by columns of assault craft hitting several related beaches simultaneously. Defenders were rendered more confused by the use of rivers and creeks to land units to the rear. Infiltration, rather than confrontation, was widely practised.

Experience in China had led to the building of the first-ever large, multi-purpose assault ship in the *Shinshu Maru*. Also, the finest naval air arm in the world was developed.

To ensure air supremacy, the first target was air bases. Immense damage resulted at Pearl Harbor, in the Philippines and in Malaya. Following-up immediately were invasion forces, the first wave starting from Formosa (Taiwan) and a compliant French Indo-China (Vietnam) and Siam (Thailand).

ABOVE: **Japanese infantry going ashore from Daihatsu landing craft. These vessels looked primitive, but were inexpensive to build and highly versatile.**

LEFT: **Japanese infantry using one-man inflatables to cross a river on the Malayan peninsula during the invasion in 1942.**

Having lost command of the air, the Allied forces had difficulty in using their considerable sea power to counter enemy moves in what was a vast theatre of war.

Moving steadily down the Malayan peninsula toward Singapore, and with the Philippines captured, the Japanese launched the second-wave attack. Always moving under air cover launched from newly captured airfields, they initiated assaults at west and north Borneo from both Indo-China and the Philippines. This was followed by multi-targeted landings against south Borneo, Celebes (Sulawesi), Ambon, Sumatra and along the so-called "Malay Barrier".

Allied morale collapsed early and totally in the face of relentless Japanese progress. Landings were in limited strength but always unpredictable for either location or time.

With the Allied forces spread so thinly in such a vast area, little or no resistance was met, and the Japanese simply regrouped and advanced. The powerful carrier group that had ravaged Pearl Harbor, followed up with the Bay of Bengal, Ceylon (Sri Lanka) and Darwin, and became free to assist in the latter phases of the campaign.

By the end of February 1942 it was all over, a triumphant vindication of manoeuvre warfare. Japan controlled all that it had desired, the "Greater East Asia Co-Prosperity Sphere" stretching from Burma in the west, and to the Gilberts in the east.

In so great an area, Japanese lines of communication were stretched to the limit and, like those of the Allies before, were vulnerable to interdiction. As Allied forces regathered military strength, retribution was only a matter of time.

LEFT: **After landing infantry and establishing a beachhead, the Imperial Japanese Army swiftly landed armour, artillery and transport vehicles. Japanese light tanks were almost useless against Allied armour.**

Operation "Jubilee", Dieppe

ABOVE: **Assault troops transfering from a Fairmile B-type Motor Launch (ML).**
LEFT: **The landing beach from a German defensive point located on a cliff. Beyond the relatively low sea wall is a wide, open space covered by a continuous line of reinforced, defended buildings.**

On August 19, 1942 the small French port of Dieppe was the focus of a major Allied raid. The intention was to hold the town for a few hours before withdrawing. Although the plan was driven by powerful political imperatives, the military objectives included:

• Testing planning, command and control procedures.
• Gauging likely German reaction to a surprise assault.
• Provoking a major air battle with the *Luftwaffe*.

Dieppe was within operational range of English south-coast airfields, on which the RAF had concentrated some 60 squadrons of fighter aircraft. Most of the 6,000 assault personnel were drawn from the 1st Canadian Army, which had yet to see action. The remainder comprised three British commandos, two of them Army, one Royal Marine.

The operation was started on July 7, but was aborted due to poor flying conditions over the Channel and Dieppe. This may well have compromised the second attempt.

Dieppe is situated in a dip in the continuous line of near-vertical chalk cliffs that form that part of the Normandy coast. It is thus dominated by high ground to either side and to the

rear. Enemy gun batteries and emplacments on these heights commanded both town and seaward approaches. A planned proposal to seize these locations with paratroops was abandoned as being too weather-dependent.

The plan was to mount a frontal assault on the town, preceded by double assaults on either flank to neutralize the gun batteries. The town was fronted by a sea wall, backed by a promenade, wide ornamental gardens and a boulevard of substantial buildings, many reinforced as strongpoints. Plans to bomb the latter before the landing were vetoed in favour of on-demand naval support gunfire. Major warships could not be risked, so this was limited mainly to the 4in guns of eight Royal Navy Hunt-class destroyers.

An armada of 237 vessels, including 188 amphibious assault craft, carried 4,961 Canadian troops and 1,057 British commandos. The approach, early on August 19, was betrayed when vessels for the left-flank landings encountered an enemy convoy. The ensuing battle scattered the LCAs and alerted the garrison ashore. Despite a valiant effort the left-flank landings were a failure. In contrast, the right-flank landings were a total success.

At 05:20 the frontal assault went in on time, against defenders by now fully alert and untroubled by the pre-assault bombardment. The Germans laid a continuous hail of fire on the beach, cutting down the Canadian troops even as they left the LCAs. The Canadians should have been supported directly by medium tanks, but the LCTs carrying these were delayed by over 10 minutes. During this short space of time, the attack lost initial momentum, which was never recovered.

The troops remained pinned-down on the steep, shingle beach. Twenty-seven tanks were eventually landed, but only 19 succeeded in getting beyond the sea wall. These were

LEFT: **The first small British tank landing craft was originally called an MLC. The LCM (1) was superseded by the LCM (3). It was designed to be handled by davits, and could be hoisted part-loaded.**
BELOW: **The raiders having withdrawn, the Germans are clearing the beach of casualties. Many of the Churchill tanks were immobilized by the soft shingle beach.**

then unable to progress into the town because of concrete obstacles. These, in turn, could not be destroyed by sappers owing to heavy enemy fire, which the tanks were unable to suppress. Gunfire from the tanks and the destroyers made little impression on the German defences.

An impasse resulted, but the military commander, offshore in a destroyer, misjudged the situation due to poor communications. He committed his floating reserve, which merely added to the numbers pinned down on the beach. By 09:00, however, the hopelessness of the situation had become apparent and, some two hours earlier than planned, a general

withdrawal was signalled. Naval craft took a terrible pounding as they beached, but succeeded in lifting nearly 1,000 survivors. By any standard, Dieppe was a disaster. Some 2,200 troops were taken prisoner. Of only 1,620 Canadians returning unwounded, approximately 1,000 had not landed. A quarter of the commandos had become casualties. Naval losses were a destroyer, 33 landing craft and 550 casualties.

The RAF had fought the air battle it had sought but, in destroying 48 of the *Luftwaffe*, it lost 106 aircraft. Having suffered under 600 casualties, the Germans were understandably jubilant at their considerable success.

Operation "Watchtower", Guadalcanal

The devastating loss of four aircraft carriers at Midway meant that any further Japanese military advance would probably require the provision of land-based air cover. With New Guinea proving to be a difficult campaign, the Japanese were keen to hold the Solomons, to act as a defensive barrier against any planned US forces counter-strike. Japanese lines of communication were by now, however, stretched to the limit, and their presence in the Solomons was sparse, with the nearest major base being at Rabaul, some 966km/600 miles distant from the most southerly islands. Considerable risk thus attended the establishment of a reconnaissance flying boat base at Tulagi and an airfield at Lunga Point on Guadalcanal, 32km/20 miles away.

Despite equally meagre resources, US forces were keen to take the offensive in the Solomons. The news, on July 5, 1942, that the enemy was constructing an airfield, triggered firm action for, once complete, this base would give the Japanese local air superiority. The improvised nature of the resulting operation,

codenamed "Watchtower", resulted in the more popular name of "Shoestring". A total of 19,000 US Marines were drawn from regiments and battalions of different divisions and units, many without recent training. The force was embarked in 19 transports, with eight cruisers and 15 destroyers for escort and fire support. Bound for both Tulagi and Guadalcanal, all amphibious forces were commanded by Rear-Admiral Richmond K. Turner.

Direct air support was provided by three aircraft carriers, operating independently under Vice-Admiral Frank Fletcher.

Following an unopposed bombardment of the Lunga Point beaches, the first US forces amphibious operation since 1898 began early on August 7. Due to the forthcoming North African landings (Operation "Torch") taking precedence, no specialist landing ships could be allocated. Ship-to-shore movement was handled by a fleet of 36ft Higgins boats, 36ft Landing Craft, Personel, Ramped (LCP [R]), and 45 and 56ft Landing Craft, Mechanized (LCM). The Japanese forces, mainly being

ABOVE: **Although popularly known as Operation "Shoestring", 15 transports were deployed for the Guadalcanal landing, with a further eight for Tulagi. The powerful naval force was little used initially.**
RIGHT: **With very limited tidal range, this beach at Guadacanal allowed New Zealand troops to exit from the LCP (R)s almost at the jungle edge.**

construction and engineering personnel, offered negligible
resistance. Beach congestion proved to be a major problem
but, by dark, 11,000 US Marines were ashore and the airfield
safely secured. Anticipated to be an easier target, Tulagi was
allocated only three battalions of US Marines. Outnumbered,

the 1,500 Japanese operating the flying boat facility were,
however, well prepared. Less than 100 were to survive the
ensuing vicious hand-to-hand combat.

Aircraft from Fletcher's carriers broke up several
determined enemy air attacks and, by the evening of
August 8, for the loss of one transport, both Tulagi and
Guadalcanal appeared to be secure. Having given just
36 hours of air cover, Fletcher then moved his force away,
anxious lest his irreplaceable carriers became targets for
submarines. The Lunga Point airfield (soon to be renamed
Henderson Field) was not yet operational, while
most of the transport ships remained half unloaded.

Meanwhile, moving at speed down the Solomons
chain from Rabaul was a powerful Japanese naval force
under Vice-Admiral Gunichi Mikawa. Although sighted
by US reconnaissance aircraft, this potent threat was
misreported and misinterpreted.

In the early hours of August 9, in a powerful hit-and-run attack,
Mikawa surprised and savaged the covering force, sinking four
cruisers off Savo Island. Mikawa's force immediately withdrew,
concerned that dawn would bring retribution in the shape of
Fletcher's aircraft. He need not have worried, but his instinct to
pull out prevented his force falling upon the now-defenceless
amphibious transports. He thus failed to achieve his main
objective, and "Watchtower" was saved.

To the US military, Guadalcanal became, like Verdun or
El Alamein, a symbolic line in the sand. The Japanese were
equally determined to recapture it and, for six months, both
sides poured in reinforcements. It was the catalyst for six
major and many lesser battles between the opposing fleets.

In an attritional campaign such as this, US forces would,
inevitably, be the victors. Finally admitting defeat, and that
the long advance had reached its limit, Japan suddenly
withdrew its troops in February 1943. Overall losses
had been two battleships, three carriers, 12 cruisers,
25 destroyers and at least 25,000 lives.

ABOVE: **The characteristic rounded stern identifies this LCM as a 45ft Mark 2,
and is from the the transport USS *Aurelia* (AKA-23). The light tank is an M3.
The later M3A1 was very effective against Japanese armour.**

LEFT: **Five British assault convoys alone (this is KMF I) involved 156 merchant ships and 52 escorts. Sailing directly from the USA were another four convoys, comprising a further 200 vessels.**

Operation "Torch", North Africa

Despite the trauma of the Japanese attack on Pearl Harbor, President Roosevelt adhered to a policy of "Germany first". For this he also overruled opposition from his Chiefs of Staff, who then, once recommitted to a major operation in the European theatre, pushed hard for an early cross-Channel assault. The experienced British, well aware that the US Army lacked battle experience, condemned this ambition as foolhardy. Roosevelt heeded their council, instructing General George C. Marshall and Admiral Ernest J. King to prepare plans for the invasion of North Africa by, at the latest, the end of October 1942. Just three months ahead.

Marshall appointed Lieutenant General Dwight D. Eisenhower as Commander-in-Chief (C-in-C), Expeditionary Force, North Africa. Admiral Andrew B. Cunningham, RN was sent to Washington to liaise at the highest level as Commander, Allied Naval Forces. Vice-Admiral Bertram Ramsay, RN headed the Anglo-American planning staff based in London.

Although the British 8th Army had been battling Italian forces and the German *Afrika Korps* since June 1940, their war had been confined to Libya and Egypt. Morocco, Algeria and Tunisia remained under the control of Vichy French authorities, in accordance with the terms of the armistice agreed with Germany in 1940. The coastline of these territories is some 2,414km/1,500 miles in length and there was considerable disagreement on where the Allied force should strike, assuming that the Germans would immediately use this as a pretext to occupy all Vichy territory.

The British wanted to land at Bizerta and Tunis, at the far eastern end, in order to thwart rapid German reinforcement from Sicily. Uncharacteristically, the US military vetoed this as too bold and simultaneous assaults were ordered at Casablanca, on the exposed Atlantic coast, and at Oran, the French naval base, also at Algiers. Forces landing at Algiers were charged with then progressing rapidly 644km/400 miles eastward to secure Tunis.

Up to 120,000 well-equipped French troops were known to be deployed in Morocco and Algeria but it was not known how hard they would resist in the name of Vichy. Allied forces numbers therefore reflected this strength – 19,500 troops for

LEFT: **Air-defence gun crews watching as assault craft move up for the Casablanca landing. Considerable opposition was encountered from warships of the Vichy French Navy.**

Casablanca, 39,000 for Oran and 43,000 for Algiers. Very widely separated the three operations had to be autonomous. The Landing Ship, Tank (LST) was not yet available so, following ship-to-shore assault with LCAs and LCMs carried by the transports, port facilities would be quickly captured in order to land armour and heavy equipment. Aircraft carriers, ever in short supply, could give early air cover but would need to be quickly withdrawn, so the early capture of airfields was essential.

Under Rear-Admiral Henry Kent Hewitt, the Casablanca operation consisted of US forces and was staged directly from the eastern seaboard of the United States. It comprised three assaults, one at Fedhala, aimed at the capital, another at Safi around 241km/150 miles to the south and another at Port Lyautey, some 97km/60 miles to the north.

Landings were timed for the early hours of November 8, 1942. Darkness was preferred by the military, with no preliminary bombardment to either alert or antagonize the French. The beach landings were executed in conditions of heavy Atlantic surf and many LCPs were swamped and lost. Only the lightest of enemy resistance spared the struggling troops from suffering heavy losses.

At Casablanca port, shore batteries were troublesome and French naval units opened fire, only to be knocked out by heavy US Navy covering fire, assisted by aircraft from five small carriers. After three days of hostilities, and in the face of a large US build-up, the French, honour satisfied, cooperated fully in bringing Casablanca back to an operational port. Already delayed offshore, however, several loaded transports had been attacked and sunk by U-boats.

To the south, Safi had been selected as being a small port with a jetty suitable for unloading armour. Beach assaults here were accordingly preceded by the port being attacked by two old destroyers, carrying 400 assault troops. With just one casualty, the force seized the facilities and, by the afternoon, a converted train ferry was discharging tanks.

Port Lyautey had an all-weather airfield, which the French resolutely defended. The build-up, already hampered by heavy surf, was delayed further by air attacks and shore-battery fire, obliging the transports to be anchored further offshore. On November 10, therefore, another old destroyer was used to

ABOVE: **Although the AKA was an "attack cargo ship", the type also carried a large number of troops and equipment.**

crash the boom on the neighbouring river and navigate the shoal water to deposit another assault group at a point close to the airfield. Its capture followed quickly, and it was soon being used by US Army Air Force fighter aircraft.

The operations against Oran and Algiers were British-run and staged directly from Great Britain. Both enjoyed distant cover from the Gibraltar-based Force 'H' of the Royal Navy, deployed to meet any major counter-attack by the Italian Navy. Of this force, fortunately, there was to be no sign.

The Oran operation, too, involved three beaches, two being around 40km/25 miles on the flanks. Again with no preliminary bombardment, the assault force began to go ashore soon after 01:00 on November 8. Sand bars and strong currents made it difficult to steer the LCAs, but opposition was negligible and the landings proceeded in an almost textbook fashion. A noteworthy contribution was made by the three British "Maracaibos", a forerunner of the LST which were designed to land armour over the beach.

LEFT: **A Landing Craft, Mechanized (LCM 594) loaded with stores and light artillery heads toward the beach at Algiers. The Royal Navy played a major role in Operation "Torch".**

In Oran, however, there was disaster. To prevent the mass scuttling of ships and demolition in the French naval port of Mers-el-Kebir, and to seize the threatening shore batteries, a US assault force was embarked on two British ships. In an operation heavily criticized before the event, the ships were to break the defending boom before off-loading the assault forces at the far end of the harbour.

For some reason the ships were not ordered in until 03:00, by which time the French were on high alert. For nearly 3.2km/2 miles the ships were expected to run the gauntlet of point-blank fire from hostile French warships. Neither ship succeeded, both being destroyed with over 50 per cent casualties. Oran and the airfields were, nonetheless, in Allied hands within 48 hours.

ABOVE: **US troops landing on the beach at Sureouf some 32km/20 miles from Algiers. Operation "Torch" signalled the entry of the USA into the war in the Mediterranean.**

The Algiers landings were notable in having senior officers embarked in specially equipped headquarters ships, notably HMS *Bulolo* which became the model for the design of subsequent US Navy AGC ships.

In this second British-controlled operation, two beaches were assaulted by US troops and one by a British unit. The landings, again in the small hours of November 8, attracted little opposition from shore batteries. British artillery observation officers had, however, been embedded in various units and these, in radio contact with fire support ships, were able to call down effective counter-fire. Again, inadequate training resulted in severe losses of assault craft. Unwieldy and under-powered at best, these required careful handling.

The harbour at Algiers was also to be attacked using two old destroyers carrying teams charged with securing the port. One, breaking the boom at the third attempt, succeeded in entering the port and landing the troops, only for all to be captured. Unable to assist, and now unsupported from ashore, the other destroyer was withdrawn but, severely damaged, sank the next day.

LEFT: **While in Casablanca port, the incomplete French battleship *Jean Bart* was heavily damaged by gunfire from USS *Massachusetts* (BB-59) and US Navy dive-bombers from USS *Ranger* (CV-4).**

French resistance in Algiers ceased on the evening of the landing and a general armistice with the Vichy Force was agreed on November 10. The four-month drive by Allied forces to Tunis had already commenced.

The generally light opposition encountered allowed many lessons to be learned cheaply. Use dedicated teams to move materiel as it was landed. Land materiel in the order in which it will be required. Designate beaches clearly, remembering that smoke screens that shielded the landing craft also blinded and disorientated coxswains. Check, and if possible, obtain up-to-date hydrographic data, offshore sandbars and inshore currents. Even the moderate Mediterranean tidal range, played havock with plans. The troops carried only essential equipment allowing the rapid turnaround of landing craft.

ABOVE: **Part of the massive convoy of 500 ships which transported troops and equipment from the USA laying at anchor off Algiers in November, 1943.**

LEFT: **Because the beach landings were virtually unopposed, many useful lessons were easily learned. Enemy air attacks on offshore shipping did, however, cause significant losses. A number of vessels at Casablanca were attacked and sunk by submarines.**

Planning an amphibious operation

An early problem for planners is calculating the level of opposition that will need to be overcome. Superior headquarters will have defined the objective, but necessary knowledge of the enemy's strength, defensive positions and capability must be gauged through intelligence or covert operations by advance forces. It is important that this stage, while thorough, must be conducted without raising the least suspicion of an alert enemy.

Major maritime powers may then be able to allocate forces suitable for the task. Lesser powers may well have to decide at this point whether to proceed.

Unless, as in World War II, amphibious operations have become repetitive, considerable lead time is required. While the necessary shipping is procured and assembled, thorough training must be undertaken. Opposed landings offer a uniquely challenging experience, particularly for the initial

ABOVE: **USS *Missouri* (BB-63) bombarding Chongjin, Korea, October 1950. Plentiful naval gunfire was both effective and good for the morale of troops.**

TOP: **Cartographers and model makers produced accurate representations of targets.** ABOVE: **Note how the later waves of assault craft lacked the tight formation of the leaders, which were guided by a line of support craft. The effect of bombardment and the lack of heavy-calibre defensive fire are evident.**

waves of troops and the naval crews of the assault craft. All need to understand, through realistic rehearsal, what will be expected of them on the day.

By their very nature, amphibious operations tend to be complex but, as complexity and confusion go together, simplicity should be ruthlessly pursued in planning. It may, however, be necessary to complicate the timetable through the use of diversionary feints or flanking operations. Limited raids might be at night, but a major landing will probably commence at dawn, following a night approach.

Timetables have to be precise and controlled by "marshals", so that each element moves as required, coordinated, for instance, with incursions by spearhead forces or with a preliminary bombardment. Within this precision, however, there must be scope for a degree of flexibility for, as has so often been stated, "no plan survives the first contact with the enemy". Planners, therefore, should continually ask themselves "What if …?" and not be afraid to face the response robustly.

For operations targeted at specific objectives, the choice of landing site may be limited. A beach should, if possible, have a gentle slope. Too shallow an angle will cause landing craft to ground too far from the water's edge, resulting in the swamping of vehicles and perhaps the drowning of heavily laden troops. Too steep an angle will result in mobility problems for vehicles, with assault craft more easily being driven broadside on to the beach by breaking seas. Ideally, a landing will be timed for a rising tide, minimising the distance that first-wave troops have to cover before finding protection, yet allowing assault craft to quickly float clear to release space on the shoreline. An advantage is the provision of a safe withdrawal area for the essential repair of ships and other craft.

Routes inland from the landing site should be adequate to allow personnel and equipment to clear the danger of the beach zone without undue delay. Assault helicopters and air

LEFT: **President Roosevelt being briefed on proposed landing sites on the Japanese mainland by General MacArthur, Admiral Nimitz and Admiral Leahy in 1944.**
BELOW: **A US Navy Chance-Vought F4U-5 Corsair overflying Inchon, Korea. Note the Iowa-class battleship USS *Missouri* (BB-63) and chartered commercial vessels still in company colours.**

cushion vehicles facilitate rapid progress inland to avoid as far as possible further "Omaha"-type situations, where a beach foothold is won but held only at an inordinate cost in casualties.

Should follow-on equipment need to be discharged from ships, it is essential that these are "combat-loaded" to ensure that these supplies are delivered ashore in the order in which they will be required.

With overall responsibility until the moment of touchdown, the navy will require resources sufficient to prevent enemy naval attack. It will already have conducted covert surveys, and either swept or marked mine-free areas.

Local maritime superiority must be matched by at least a "favourable air situation". If this involves the commitment of invaluable aircraft carriers, the requirement for the early capture of an airfield is obvious.

A headquarters ship, with enhanced communication equipment, will accommodate the commander of the amphibious task force (usually naval), commander landing

force (army or marines) and the air-control officer. Calls for gunfire support will also need to be allocated to specific ships. Inter-service harmony is, at this point, of paramount importance.

LEFT: **If transport is the key to an army's fighting options, then fuel becomes as important as ammunition. More operations by LSTs were devoted to cargo and personnel than to carrying tanks.**

LEFT: **USS** *Pocono* **(ACG-16), an Andirondack-class amphibious force command ship. The vessel was launched on January 25, 1945, and was stricken from the Naval Vessel Register in December 1971.**

Command and Control (C2)

Planning for an amphibious operation will have been structured around the means of achieving a clearly (it is to be hoped) designated objective. For a multinational organization such as NATO it is a prerequisite that the governments contributing elements to an Amphibious Task Force (ATF) will all have been working toward that common objective. This cannot be taken for granted for there may be, for instance, problems in inter-operability, logistics, and variations in doctrine, rules of engagement and, even, political bias. A further edge is added to this combination by the necessary involvement of naval, air, army and marine components.

The traditional starting point for amphibious force command was to view it as a naval operation leading to a military operation. Both parts being of equal importance in the realization of the objective, it appeared correct to appoint separate naval and military commanders usually, but not always, of equal rank. With cooperation, such arrangements could work well but, sometimes, inter-service friction became an issue (such as at Gallipoli and, disastrously, Norway in 1940) to the detriment of the operation.

Currently, it is more usual that the Commander, Amphibious Task Force (CATF) is naval, reflecting that service's prominent role. The Commander, Land Forces (CLF) will, by definition, enjoy equal status but, until his forces are ashore, coordination and final decision making are the responsibility of the CATF.

Ideally, in peacetime, the commanders and their staffs should work and train together within a common and permanent organization. This requires frequent exercises as, for instance, combat-equipped troops do not usually expect to embark and disembark in small craft, while armour and heavy equipment is hardly designed to be easily off-loaded over an open beach. For preference, a landing will be planned so as to be unopposed, but the location will probably be determined largely by the choice of objective. Exercises will expose the control limitations imposed by the range of communications and data processing equipment available on the designated command flagship.

Much will necessarily devolve upon subordinate commanders, as the force must travel and operate within the envelope of local superiority. The longer the passage,

RIGHT: **USS** *Blue Ridge* **(LCC-19) has been in US Navy service since 1970. The vessel is equipped with satellite communications equipment. The ship was the command flagship in Operation "Desert Shield" and "Desert Storm" from August 1990 to April 24, 1991.**

LEFT: **USS *Wright* (CC-2) was originally built as a Saipan-class aircraft carrier. In 1962, the vessel was converted to function as a mobile command post, for top-echelon commanders and staff, and equipped with facilities for worldwide communications.**

as in the Pacific during World War II, the larger the force becomes, as the support forces themselves require support in the form of fuel, stores and ammunition.

As a minimum, Anti-Submarine (AS) and Anti-Air (AA) forces, together with a Surface Action Group (SAG) require to be attached. These may need to be drawn from separate commands, and may give rise to problems if not placed under the control of the CATF (e.g. Fletcher's carrier force for "Watchtower" and Patton's command ship during "Torch").

For the CLF, the post-landing experience may be liberating, for he will assume overall responsibility and if, for instance, his force is in brigade strength, he is no longer answerable to divisional control. As with all competent commanders, the CLF must have the qualities of judgement and flexibility, for the reality of the situation once ashore will rarely meet with expectations, however good the

planning and the preliminary information gathered by intelligence. The enemy will adapt to circumstance, and the CLF must be ready to respond appropriately.

Judgement by both senior commanders is essential in deciding at which point centralized control is to be devolved downward. Tactical decisions are best made by commanders on the spot (note the disastrous dispersal of convoy PQ 17 in 1942 on orders from London). To quote the official manual, "effective command and control must comprise directions at the highest level necessary to achieve unity of purpose, combined with a delegation of responsibility to the lowest level commensurate with the most appropriate and effective use of resources". If effective Command and Control (C2) is vital to success, it follows that the new military science of Command and Control Warfare (C2W) is equally valuable by degrading the capability of the enemy.

ABOVE: **A view of the Joint Operations Room on board USS *Ancon* (AGC-4). Command personnel are at their stations surrounded by maps and status boards.**

ABOVE: **Another view of the Joint Operations Room on USS *Ancon* (AGC-4), from where the invasion of Sicily was controlled on July 3, 1943.**

The amphibious force

World War II was the proving ground on which amphibious warfare came of age. Everything since has been a refinement of what then took place during the many seaborne operations undertaken during the conflict.

Isolated, and facing an occupied continental Europe, Great Britain began modestly with raids, but entertained the idea that Europe would eventually be invaded and liberated. Still under the threat of invasion, she developed concepts for specialist craft, the orders for which were placed in a still-neutral USA. These programmes were to take time to enter production. The British, meanwhile, used LSIs of sizes ranging from converted steam packets to modern cargo liners. The common specification was for troop accommodation and heavy davits under which were slung assault landing craft (LCA/LCVP).

Here were embodied the two major categories of amphibious warfare vessel – the Landing Ships (LSI, LST, LSD, etc.) intended to make a "shore-to-shore" open-sea transit, and the Landing Craft (LCT, LCU, LCVP, etc.) designed to function on arrival in the "ship-to-shore" mode.

Successive landings raised the requirement for further specialist craft, particularly rocket- or gun-armed support craft to accompany the first assault. Not capable of long ocean passages, smaller craft such as these would join the main assault force from intermediate locations, as with the landings in North Africa and on Sicily.

On the day, there were never sufficient assault landing craft, DUKW amphibious trucks or tracked landing vehicles (LVT). This gave rise to the design for the LPD, effectively a powered floating dock capable of accommodating many small vessels in a docking well for an ocean passage.

Such a ship could also stow a lesser number of larger craft, each pre-loaded with stores or transport. Should the LPD then be extended with storage for further vehicles and/or accommodation for a troop contingent, the type would become the more capable

ABOVE: **The combined carrier/amphibious force is formidable, but in such a neat formation is vulnerable to a tactical nuclear strike.**

LSD. With the general introduction of helicopters for assault or materiel transfer, a flight deck and hangar naturally followed, necessitating a radical rearrangement from which emerged the virtually self-contained LHD.

World War II amphibious operations were won with large numbers of basic vessels that were simple to the point of crudeness, leading to reasonable criticism of the current "all-eggs-in-one-basket" approach of the hugely expensive LHD and derivatives.

In today's major operation, an Amphibious Task Group (ATG) will be only one component of an Amphibious Task Force (ATF), which will include a carrier group,

ABOVE: **Naval air power has become a vital part of an amphibious assault. Here, an FJ-4 Fury is being launched as another is moving forward. An F2H-2 Banshee is being positioned on the starboard catapult, ready for launch.**

ABOVE: **A nuclear-powered attack submarine, such as the French** *Amethyste*, **is an essential component for the defence of an amphibious task force.**
RIGHT: **The helicopter is now an essential part of an amphibious operation, in the first instance to land troops, and then to deliver stores and reinforcements.**

nuclear-powered attack submarine and a logistics group of "one-stop" tanker/ammunition/stores ships. A further development is the pre-positioning ship, usually with Roll-on, Roll-off (Ro-Ro) facilities and heavy lifting gear for cargo. This is loaded with heavy, follow-up equipment including armour, and may be held in forward areas for a considerable time.

Complete with various escort screens, an ATF becomes a very large formation which, in the satellite age, is impossible to conceal. It must, therefore, proceed within a protective "cocoon", with escorts providing anti-submarine, anti-air, anti-surface cover and even anti-space attack cover.

Denied concealment, the force must rely even more on deception or disruptive procedures to disguise the time and place of the planned strike. Ideally, it will not be placed within sight of the enemy's shore (except, perhaps as a show of strength in a time of tension) but use high-speed assault craft to operate from Over The Horizon (OTH).

The Landing Craft, Air Cushion (LCAC) is currently the US forces key asset, its size, rather than those of the earlier LCU, determining the docking well dimensions of the major amphibious warfare ship. With a loaded speed

of 40 knots (71kph), and limited over-land capability, it might permit a major shift in procedure whereby, using suitable topography, the LCAC would be used in combination with assault helicopters or tilt-wing aircraft to strike suddenly behind a defended shoreline. Analogous to earlier pre-emptive paratroop landings, such "hook" attacks would avoid the requirement for an initial "traditional" type of frontal assault.

ABOVE: **Part of the Falklands invasion force – hospital ships** *Uganda* **and** *Hydra* **refuelling from RFA** *Olmeda*. LEFT: **RFA** *Fort Austin* **(A386), a stores and ammunition carrier, with repair ship RFA** *Diligence* **(A132) alongside.**

Pre-landing operations

In these days of satellite surveillance, it is difficult to envisage an operation against a technologically sophisticated opponent achieving surprise unless mounted over a short distance and supported by effective deception. Pre-landing operations must, therefore, be a fine balance between a beneficial contribution to the assault and maintenance of tactical surprise.

Diversionary and preparatory activities might considerably pre-date an assault and, as they may involve separate commands (even at higher command level) good personal relationships are helpful. Although technology has advanced since World War II, basic requirements here have remained the same.

Observation, intelligence or pure habit may indicate whether the defence will oppose the landing on the beach, or nullify a pre-assault bombardment by counter-attacking as the invaders move inland. In the first case, Naval Gunfire Support (NGS) and close-air support need to be closely coordinated up to and beyond the moment of touchdown. In the latter, preparations would be directed to making it difficult for the defence to move further reinforcements into the area. Historically, in an operation as large as that in Normandy, both approaches were found necessary.

World War II first saw the introduction of specialist teams of divers/combat swimmers to gather intelligence. Measurements of beach gradients and the disposition of obstructions gathered by them will be critical to the successful grounding of assault craft on the day; monitoring of tidal range may influence time and date; analysis of beach material is essential for the benefit of vehicles (at Dieppe in 1942, for instance, many tanks immediately shed tracks on landing due to the size of the shingle). Items of divers' equipment might be "lost" on alternative beaches in the interests of deception.

Mines laid in the surf zone are likely to have a short life, but detecting and countering is not easy. Removing by hand may be required, following a covert survey by a submarine-launched

ABOVE: **Royal Navy X-craft (midget submarines) landed divers to assess the load-bearing qualities of the Normandy beaches. Later, the vessels were used as fixed guidance beacons during the landings.**

ABOVE: **An air reconnaissance photograph of a Normandy beach at low tide. The obstructions were given names such as "Rommel's Asparagus" "Belgian Gate" or "Czech Hedgehogs".**

ABOVE: **Underwater Demolition Teams (UDT) remain invaluable in the clearance of paths through approaches with obstacles.**

ABOVE: **Forward observer teams are among the first ashore, with the task of supplying naval gunners with precise coordinates for close-support gunfire.**

LEFT: **Ports along the south coast of England were used as loading points for D-Day, June 6, 1944. Here at Weymouth, Dorset, troops can be seen loading stores and vehicles into a variety of vessels ready for landing on Omaha beach.**

Autonomous Underwater Vehicle (AUV). With the AUV recovered by the submarine, and the stored data downloaded and analysed, a specialist clearance team will be positioned by Swimmer Delivery Vehicle (SWD).

A World War II assault might be preceded by parachute and/or glider landings to secure vital bridgeheads to prevent enemy reinforcement and also to facilitate eventual breakout from the beachhead. Such procedures are still valid, although given further flexibility with the availability of assault helicopters and aircraft such as the tilt-rotor Bell Boeing MV-22B Osprey aircraft, now in service with the US Marine Corps.

The army prefers to attack at night but, in confined waters, the navy needs to see the target. Commonly, therefore, an approach will be in darkness, leading to an assault at first light.

Several World War II landings saw groups of assault craft hit the wrong beaches. In any but the simplest of approaches, therefore, a duty of the covert landing teams will be to lay dormant electronic beacons. By interrogating these ahead of the first wave, marshalling craft will be accurately positioned, providing a "gate" through which the assault wave will pass.

Pacific or "Torch"-sized amphibious groups relied, if necessary, on the massive firepower of the covering force to get to the objective in the face of major opposition. Particularly with the advent of ship-killing kamikaze aircraft, this tended to concentrate the formation. During the Cold War, however, this trend was firmly abandoned with the advent of tactical nuclear weapons. A single, nuclear-armed missile, launched at considerable range from an aircraft, submarine or surface ship, could now devastate a whole formation, making dispersion essential. Being used at sea, such low-yield weapons would not directly affect civilian populations and might not be considered as precipitating an all-out nuclear confrontation.

Future conflict may well be decided, not on the quality of fighting men, but on which side acquires superior technology.

ABOVE: **A platoon deploying from an assault craft, in single file to avoid bunching.**
LEFT: **A D-Day exercise by US Rangers, probably at Bude, Cornwall. A rocket grapnel has been fired while a medic attends to a "casualty".**

LEFT: **Reinforcements pouring on to Omaha beach after the D-Day landing. A Rhino ferry (RHF-19) loaded with troops and artillery is being manoeuvered into position by a bulldozer.**

Securing the beachhead and breaking out

An amphibious assault is but one phase, the means of creating a beachhead ("lodgement") which can be enlarged and consolidated prior to breakout. While an unopposed landing is desirable, it may not be possible because it may place the invaders too far from their objective (the 1982 Falklands campaign provides an example of fine judgement). During the Pacific war, most island objectives were so small that every beach was defendable.

As the first waves go in, the operation is at its most vulnerable. Preferably, the defenders will be recovering from a preparatory bombardment that, having just lifted, has shifted to the flanks and rear. Hopefully, they will be preparing for an attack by airborne forces landing in the rear. Today, these

might well have been mounted from Over The Horizon (OTH), by troops in helicopters and LCACs.

Supported by light, amphibious armour the first waves will endeavour to push ahead over the cratered shoreline, creating a measure of space, albeit still under fire. At the direction of the landing force commander, larger landing craft carrying additional armour, artillery and engineer units will be ordered to land. It should be emphasized how important it is to establish a momentum, to create a balanced force ashore capable

BELOW: **A Beach, Armoured Recovery Vehicle (BARV), one of Hobart's "funnies", is being used to recover a Bedford OXC tractor unit and trailer from a beach in Normandy on June 14, 1944.**

LEFT: **After the Omaha beachhead was established on June 6, 1944, US Navy communication posts were set up, where radio, signal lamps and even flags (semaphore) were used to contact vessels at sea.**

of holding off an opponent who is already rushing in reinforcements. On the result of this action, the survival of the beachhead will hang, and the tactical commander will have sought to acquire space, or freedom of manoeuvre will be denied him. He should, by this stage, have been able to transfer his headquarters ashore.

During the expansion of the beachhead, supplies and reinforcements need to be put ashore at a rate compatible with the situation. Laden transports and cargo ships, having to loiter offshore, are vulnerable to attack (as at Guadalcanal and at Leyte) and their captains are obviously keen to offload and to move out. Early experience showed, however, that beaches receiving resources more quickly than could be distributed, rapidly became chaotic and vulnerable to air attack.

The tactical commander may need to redispose his forces in order to match them to the developing situation, but a rapid breakout ("exploitation") will normally be desirable to prevent the defence, which is blessed with the shorter lines of communication, sealing off the beachhead perimeter, neutralizing the "lodgement" until such time as a decisive counter-attack will drive it back into the sea.

Air superiority is highly desirable. There are fewer aircraft carriers in service today than during World War II. They might, as then, be used in the initial stages of the operation, but will certainly be withdrawn as quickly as possible. It is essential, therefore, that facilities for the operation of land-based air power are captured or constructed with some urgency.

An unpleasant possibility is that, while progress ashore has gone "according to plan", the enemy has been able to contest sea control, thereby hazarding, slowing and even preventing the necessary rate of build-up. The defence may then gain strength at a higher rate and the landing force commander,

anxious not be surrounded, may be moved to attempt break-out earlier than he would have wished. Already beyond the range of naval gunfire support, leading units may push ahead to the point where insufficiently secured lines of communication are in danger of being severed.

The terrain of the hinterland will have had considerable influence on the operation's logistics. The more mountainous or jungle-clad, the more that infantry will be preferable to heavy support. Reinforcement units may well be considerably larger than those of the initial assault force, and army rather than marines. They may, therefore, integrate the assault force and its command structure into their own, a situation that the original landing force commander might find difficult to accept. "His" assault, will, however, by then have developed successfully into a campaign.

BELOW: **The Landing Craft, Air Cushion (LCAC) is a fast and efficient vessel for beach landings, with the extra ability to carry vehicles beyond the beach.**

Logistics

No amount of military genius can help a tactical commander whose logistics organization cannot deliver the men and materiel that he needs. Somewhat unexciting to many, logistics will depend upon the operational plan as much as the plan depends upon logistics.

The management of shipping is complex and, in an operation of any magnitude, is best undertaken by those who are experienced. Compared with their supplies, transport and stores, troops occupy little shipping space but, conversely, require passenger shipping which is always in short supply.

Until recent times, Britain had large mercantile and fishing fleets, together with a substantial reserve of skilled seamen. In war, shipping was government-controlled, the provision of tonnage for expeditionary warfare (or trawlers for minesweeping) being a matter of allocating suitable ships. By 1982, however, the Red Ensign fleet had diminished to the point that maintaining the 12,784km/8,000-mile sea line of communication to the Falklands depended considerably upon commercial shipping. This will always be expensive to charter at short notice, and there is no guarantee of availability.

Today, Britain has virtually abandoned the merchant marine. The few ships that remain sail mostly under flags of convenience, while the long tradition of seafaring has disappeared, it being cheaper to employ seamen from the Far East.

The experience of the USA was different in that their pre-war merchant marine was small in comparison to the volume of trade. Always having depended upon foreign flagged shipping, they replaced this during both World Wars with impressive programmes of vessels built to strictly standard designs.

The steady evolution of Plan Orange had identified that, in a Pacific war with Japan, the westward advance of US forces would require an enormous "fleet train" to

ABOVE: **US Rangers loaded in LCAs waiting to be transferred out to the vessels that will carry the force to Omaha beach.**

support the battle fleet. Just how enormous was not apparent until it happened. When, in the latter stages of World War II, the British created a Royal Navy "Pacific Fleet" to assist the US Navy (USN), it arrived sadly deficient in support shipping and needed to depend upon the generosity of the USN for the replenishment necessary to keep the fleet continuously on station.

ABOVE: **Deck cargo being lifted by a mobile crane from the deck of an LST.**
LEFT: **A Multiple Gun Motor Carriage (MGMC) M16 from a mobile anti-aircaft battalion being reversed on to an LCT.**

ABOVE: **The bulldozer was cited by Admiral Halsey, USN, as being one of the three major elements crucial to success in the Pacific.** LEFT: **The pontoon bridge, here in Normandy, was a variation on the causeway (above). Note the "Gooseberry" breakwater in the distance.**

Beaching vessels, such as LSTs, speed up delivery by a reported factor of seven. The procedure, however, involves risk in a developing battle situation, where the need is for a small load to be delivered on a continuous basis.

Much modern commercial shipping carries no cargo-lifting gear, making it unsuitable until a deep-water port has been captured. Ship-to-shore movement will, in any case, require over-the-side transfer to LCVPs or LCUs, amphibious trucks and self-propelled modular pontoons, developed from the "Rhino" ferries of World War II.

Ships should be "combat-loaded", so as to discharge equipment in the correct order, with logistics specialists both aboard and in the handling parties ashore.

After 1945, the US merchant fleet again reduced rapidly, but the US Navy maintained sufficient tonnage in reserve for support. This, of course, has diminished and changed over the years but now, configured as the Military Sealift Command (MSC), has acquired considerable high-grade tonnage. Replenishment-At-Sea (RAS) has moved toward a "one-stop" operation, with a single ship supplying fuel, together with limited quantities of stores and ammunition. Transports tend to be specialized Roll-on, Roll-off (Ro-Ro) ships and container vessels. The concept of pre-loaded pre-positioning ships allows a core of essential equipment to be maintained in "hot-spots" without the need for expensive and politically sensitive foreign bases.

The Royal Fleet Auxiliary (RFA), in Britain, has received some modern purpose-built tonnage but still remains inadequate in terms of capacity. A major problem in the past was the habit of the military to retain supply ships in the operations area, using them as floating stores rather than creating large supply dumps ashore.

ABOVE: **Two British LCM (9) in distinctive Royal Marine camouflage. Note the roll-over canopy over the tank deck on the vessel in the centre. The "Mexeflote" in the distance is a self-propelled pontoon.**

LEFT: **A Norwegian fishing boat alongside a British Tribal-class destroyer during the first raid, March 1941. Two ex-Royal Dutch Mail fast motor ferries were used for the first time as LSI (M) on the raid. HMS *Queen Emma* (MV *Koningin Emma*) and HMS *Princess Beatrix* (MV *Prinses Beatrix*) would be used on many operations, including D-Day.**

Operation "Claymore", Lofoten Islands

The concept of a "commando", as an elite unit trained to use unorthodox means to harass an enemy at perceived weak points, was resurrected by Prime Minister Churchill shortly after the debacle at Dunkirk. Raising and training these battalion-sized formations took time and it was March 1941 before a significant operation could be staged.

At the approaches to Narvik in occupied Norway (already the scene of major naval actions during the previous April) were the Lofoten Islands. Isolated and difficult to reinforce quickly, these supported large fish oil processing plants, the spectacular destruction of which would both affect the German war effort while providing a useful propaganda exercise for the British.

ABOVE: **The Lofoten Islands gave the newly formed British commando force one of its first experiences of action.**

ABOVE: **Fish oil from a ruptured storage tank burning on the surface of the sea in Stamsund Harbour. The commando force encountered no organized resistance.**

LEFT: **Packed into an LCA, some of the 500 men from Nos. 3 and 4 Commando are seen here evacuating from Stamsund Harbour. Five enemy vessels were destroyed in the harbour.**

Two newly converted fast LSI (M), both ex-Dutch North Sea ferries, were used to transport the two commandos involved. Each ship carried six LCAs and two LCMs under davits. Taking leave of their heavy passage escort early on the morning of March 3, the two ships moved in under destroyer cover, with each commando divided between two objectives.

Total surprise was achieved and opposition from the small German occupying force was light. Local citizens willingly assisted in the decision-making regarding the choice of material for demolition, there being no wish to hurt Norwegian interests more than necessary.

British military equipment and the preparation of the ships involved for the Arctic proved rather less than adequate, but all fish oil stocks and facilities were destroyed, along with several small German ships. Aboard the armed trawler *Krebs* captured by the destroyer HMS *Somali*, the invaluable Enigma settings for the current period were found.

Operation "Claymore" was an early example of a raid in force, with limited objectives. The raiders were ashore for less than ten hours, achieved their objectives and returned with over 200 prisoners, 60 collaborators and over 300 Norwegian volunteers, who wished to fight on with the British.

A useful, if unforeseen, consequence was the beginning of Adolf Hitler's irrational fear that the Allies planned eventually to invade Norway.

RIGHT: **The spectacular destruction of facilities in the March raid provided perfect cover for the operation's major objective, the capture of Enigma material from a German weather trawler.**

LEFT: **A fully loaded LCM from USS** *Leonard Wood* **(APA-12) departing for the landing area.**

Operation "Husky", Sicily

On May 13, 1943, the last Axis forces surrendered in Tunisia. North Africa was clear and the next Allied attack would be against occupied Europe. A rapid move was vital in order to capitalize on the enemy's disarray, but the US military considered that any operation short of a cross-Channel thrust, aimed directly at the German heartland, would only prolong hostilities unnecessarily. The British argued the necessity of relieving pressure on the USSR and that, with over 40 divisions already in France, the Germans could deal with any cross-Channel invasion without

weakening the eastern front. Italy, they reasoned, was weakened and war-weary. Strike there, and put Italy out of the war, thus creating a vacuum which the Germans would be obliged to fill with forces drawn from the east.

Reluctantly, the US military agreed on Sicily being the next objective, and an elaborate programme of deception was begun, aimed at encouraging the enemy's own ideas which favoured landings in Greece or Sardinia. Many high-ranking German officers still considered Sicily more likely, as it was within range of air cover based in North Africa.

RIGHT: **HMSub** *Unruffled* **returning to Malta after a patrol in the Mediterranean. The vessel was used in support of Allied victories in North Africa, Sicily and Italy. During these actions 12 cargo ships and three supply schooners were sunk. An Italian heavy cruiser was also disabled, and even a freight train attacked.**

ABOVE: **Bombed by *Luftwaffe* Ju-88 aircraft on the afternoon of July 11, the Liberty ship SS *Robert Rowan* caught fire. The crew were able to abandon ship without loss of life before the cargo of ammunition exploded.**

ABOVE: **Beaches on Sicily were often of shallow incline and consisted of sand that was too soft for wheeled vehicles. Before beach matting was laid, much equipment had to be manhandled off the beach.**

They appeared even more correct when, in the ten days preceding the landings, Allied air power attacked the island, seeking to reduce Axis strength and to destroy both airfields and communications. The main force of this action was applied at the western end of the island, to reinforce the notion of a likely landing site, as it is closer to North Africa.

Originally, in fact, the US forces were to have landed in the west, but the British, scheduled to assault the southern extremity around Capo Passero, objected that their left flank would,

thereby, be left vulnerable, and that the overall Allied strength should not be quite so divided. As adopted, therefore, Operation "Husky" would still need some 115,000 mainly British and Canadian troops going ashore in the south while, to the west, around the great coastal arc between Licata and Scoglitti, some 66,000 US troops would land. Over 2,500 ships and craft were required with convoys coordinated from the United States, Britain and around the Mediterranean. A powerful British naval force would cover against any attack by the Italian navy.

LEFT: **Gliders, particularly the US-built WACO CG-4A Hadrian, were used to considerable effect in the British sector. Difficult winds, poor navigation and inexperienced pilots unfortunately resulted in a high loss rate.**

43

LEFT: **British LCT (4) and those of US forces landed short of beaches which had parallel sand bars. Few pontoon causeways were available.**

As the invasion fleet approached during the small hours of July 10, 1943, the many unwieldy LSTs and LCTs were experiencing difficulties coping with a rough sea, raised by a brisk northwest wind, which also covered beaches with a heavy surf. The beaches had a shallow slope, with offshore sandbars, so that landing craft tended to ground far from the shoreline. The US Navy had brought new floating pontoons which linked to form ship-to-shore causeways but these, unfortunately, missed the initial landings. Another innovation, the DUKW amphibious vehicle was to prove invaluable in the operation.

Near Gela, US forces spearheaded their landing by dropping some 3,000 paratroops. Although considerably scatted by the strong breeze, they were able to disrupt a determined German response to the landings. Fortunately, the army and navy commanders, Major-General George Patton and Rear-Admiral Henry Kent Hewitt, cooperated harmoniously and naval support gunfire was frequently effective in breaking up counter-attacks by enemy armoured forces.

Still experiencing heavy resistance, the US military followed up, on the following night, with a division of paratroops. The news that it would be delayed was not received by most of the ships in the amphibious fleet offshore, and when the large formation of low-flying aircraft crossed the anchorage shortly after an enemy air raid, every gunner opened fire. Over 40 of these aircraft were shot down, with considerable loss of life. Opposition to the British landings was initially light, and these were preceded by an ambitious, brigade-strength gliderborne landing to secure a vital bridge. The strong wind again caused severe problems. Over half the 130 gliders crash-landed in the sea, just seven landing in the target area. The bridge, nonetheless, was taken and held.

British command relationships worked less smoothly than those of the US force. The British appeared content with their air support but the US Navy Rear-Admiral Hewitt complained that,

BELOW: **The DUKW amphibious vehicle was used for the first time on Operation "Husky", and proved to be a valuable asset.**

ABOVE: **Newly introduced, the DUKW, or "Duck", was a six-wheel drive amphibious vehicle.** LEFT: **Men of the 51st Highland Division wading ashore from a Landing Craft, Infantry (LC [I]).**

where British carrier-based aircraft were instantly available, the system for summoning RAF support was very slow. His actual words were somewhat stronger.

The British tactical army commander, General Bernard Montgomery, later strongly criticized the scattered locations of British senior commanders: "Cunningham (Royal Navy) is in Malta; Tedder (Royal Air Force) is in Tunis; Alexander (Army) is at Syracuse. It beats me how anyone thinks you can run a campaign in that way, with the three commanders of the three services about 966km/600 miles from each other". The planning staff of General Eisenhower, the Supreme Allied Commander were, meanwhile at Algiers.

Although the Germans bemoaned the fact that the Allies could deploy superior strength by land, sea or air at will, they deployed their own remaining air power effectively. The British sector, closest to an airfield on the Italian mainland, received the most attention, with sudden raids by single aircraft or small groups which were very difficult to detect and to intercept. By now, all vessels, particularly the large and valuable LSIs, were turned around rapidly. However, new ships were continually arriving, so the enemy never lacked targets. Losses were significant.

The large British fleet providing deep cover against the absent Italian Navy was taking some damage by Italian torpedoes from aircraft and submarines. Bored with these unfulfilling duties, its commander, Vice-Admiral Sir Algernon Willis, detached single ships or groups to supplement the busy bombardment groups. As in the US sector, naval gunfire had a very considerable effect.

The occupation of Sicily, which took under six weeks, became something of a race between US forces and the British to reach Messina. Just 3.2km/2 miles across the strait from the Italian mainland, it was the obvious centre for the inevitable evacuation of Axis forces. The northern and southern coasts of Sicily, each some 274km/170 miles in length, meet at the westernmost extremity around Marsala and Trapani. The eastern coast, runs northward from the British invasion beaches some

209km/130 miles to Messina. Where US forces had to break out and secure the island's vast heartland, British and Canadian forces appeared to have the simpler task of advancing along the coastal strip. Here, however, were the larger centres of population – Syracuse, Augusta, Catania and Taormina – while between the last two loomed the mass of Mount Etna. Crossed by a number of rivers, this coastal route could be, and was, resolutely defended. The crack SS-Hermann Göring and 1st Parachute (*Fallschirmjäger*) Divisions fought a steadfast retreat, buying time for evacuation plans to be completed at Messina.

With Patton's forces greatly dependent upon the northern coast road, and Montgomery's on the eastern, the Germans were puzzled why neither used their respective amphibious forces to bypass any opposition. The US military did just twice, and to good effect. When the more conventional General Montgomery finally overcame his misgivings, the incursion came too late to be of use.

The greatest surprise of the Sicilian campaign, the successful enemy evacuation, began on August 3 when Italian troops began to be ferried across the strait. They and the Germans were given ample time to set up numerous anti-aircraft and coastal gun batteries. Coastal craft, car ferries, Siebel ferries, MFPs – all were pressed into service. But this was no panic evacuation, the Germans not beginning to cross until August 10. Six routes were used and changed from day to day. The approach roads on the Sicilian side were blocked with men and transport, yet the overwhelming Allied air superiority appeared powerless to penetrate the defensive barrage. A bold naval stroke might well have stopped the exodus totally, but Cunningham, uncharacteristically, stated that there was "no effective method, either by sea or air". At some cost in men and boats only MTBs were used to challenge the enemy by night.

Around 130,000 Axis prisoners (7,000 German) were taken, but 100,000, including 40,000 Germans, escaped. Sicily was taken but, for the Allies, much remained for improvement, particularly in inter-service and inter-allied cooperation.

Operation "Avalanche", Salerno

ABOVE: **The Sele river (centre) marked the boundary between the US beaches (left) and British (right). The choice of targets for a torpedo bomber is obvious.**

Following the Axis evacuation of Sicily the British Eighth Army waited 14 days before crossing the Strait of Messina on September 3, 1943. This move was followed, six days later, by the landing of the Allied Fifth Army, 322km/200 miles in the German rear at Salerno. It was intended thus to unbalance the enemy facing the Eighth Army by cutting lines of communication, while opening the way to the early capture of the major port, Naples.

Unusually, the Italian coastal area south of Salerno was a flat flood plain, fronted by 32km/20 miles of beaches that were very suitable for an amphibious landing. It also had considerable drawbacks, being bounded by high ground offering few exits but excellent defensive features. The location was beyond the range of most Allied fighters operating from Sicily. Intelligence, also, indicated that the area German commander, Field Marshal Albert Kesselring, fully anticipated such an Allied attack.

From German experience in North Africa and Sicily, Kesselring knew that any Allied assault would be in irresistible force. Accordingly, he arranged only nominal resistance immediate to the shoreline. Artillery was well located in the mountainous hinterland, from which every detail of the Salerno operation could be observed and shelled. Kesselring kept back the main strength of the Tenth Army, including two armoured divisions, to respond as the battlefield situation developed.

With the Italian surrender just announced, Allied troops were in something of a holiday mood. It was not to last. Until the capture of nearby Montecorvino airfield, air cover would depend upon five British escort carriers (CVE). The combination of short flight decks and insufficient speed in near-windless conditions caused hard landings, which repeatedly broke the fragile undercarriages of the Supermarine Seafire fighters. The enemy, in any case, used fighter-bombers in damaging hit-and-run raids that were almost impossible to intercept.

The US Fifth Army under Lieutenant General Mark W. Clark comprised the British X Corps, attacking north of the Sele river, and the US VI Corps, attacking to the south. The landings early on September 9, went much as planned, with immediate resistance eliminated by bold, close-in naval gunfire. Due to an acute shortage of large landing craft, however, the build-up was slow, while Kesselring's reaction was resolute and immediate.

Every Allied movement attracted artillery fire while the few tanks already ashore were insufficient to deal with powerful German armour. The key to Allied survival quickly became the Bombardment Liaison Officers (BLO) attached to various units. At their request, cruisers and destroyers fired vast quantities of ammunition at targets that were clearly visible. The Germans frequently returned fire.

ABOVE: **USS *Philadelphia* (CL-41), part of the bombardment fleet. In the background, a YMS minesweeper is laying smoke.** LEFT: **The assault craft forming up and moving to the beach. On the horizon is the mountainous hinterland of southern Italy overlooking the Salerno plain.**

LEFT: **The value of the pontoon causeway is clearly evident here, the LST being grounded on a sand ridge. The Dodge WC-54 vehicles are considerably heavier than a Jeep. Metal matting has been laid, making vehicle movement easier.**

The *Luftwaffe* responded with specialist anti-ship formations equipped with the new, radio-controlled Fritz-X glider bomb. These were highly effective but used sparingly, so that they created more apprehension than damage. Meanwhile, the barrage of naval gunfire continued. By September 13, matters were critical. The operation had not only lost momentum but was bogged down. Allied infantry was continually pitted against German armour. There was no space for a mobile reserve but there existed insufficient strength to break out.

Thwarted, Clark considered (to the disgust of his fellow commanders) abandoning half of the beachhead to reinforce the other, but settled for reinforcement by two battalions of paratroops and 1,500 fresh soldiers landed from warships.

The crisis passed and, on September 16, Kesselring admitted defeat. He had insufficient resources to dislodge the beachhead and he had been refused reinforcement from further north. To the south, the Eighth Army under Montgomery had pushed up the coast and were poised to relieve Clark's predicament. To the latter's relief, the Germans began to pull out. Naples, which had been heavily damaged, was scheduled to have been taken by September 21, but was not

occupied until October 1. In these ten days, reinforcements and equipment had to come from the beaches, creating a logistics problems that led directly to the development of the "Mulberry" artificial harbour for the D-Day landings.

ABOVE: **A Sherman III (M4-A2) about to be driven ashore on to an Italian beach. It is a command vehicle well laden with combat accessories and with a wading trunk over the hull rear.** LEFT: **Before metal matting could be laid on the beach, a great deal of equipment had to be carried to the storage areas.**

USSR

MONGOLIA

MANCHURIA

CHINA

Peking

JAPAN

Tokyo

BURMA

Hong
Kong

Okinawa
Apri 1– June 22 1945

Iwo Jima
Feb. 19–Mar. 16 1945

1945

MARIANAS

Wake
Dec. 23 1

THAILAND

FRENCH
INDOCHINA

Leyte Gulf
Oct. 24–26 1944

Bataan/Corregidor
Dec. 1941–
May 1942

PHILIPPINES

Philippine Sea
June 19–21 1944

Tinian
July 24 1944

1944

MARSH
ISLAN

Guam
July 21 1944

Eniwetok
Jan. 31 1944

1945

Ngufu
Oct. 16 1944

Kwajalein
Jan. 31 194

MALAYA

1944

Palau
Sept. 15 1944

CAROLINE ISLANDS

Singapore

BORNEO

SUMATRA

1944

SOLOMON
ISLANDS

Bismarck Sea
Mar. 2–4 1943

Guadalcanal
Aug. 7 1942–
Feb. 9 1943

Java Sea
Feb. 27–Mar. 1 1942

NEW GUINEA

Coral Sea
May 7–8 1942

JAVA

Port Moresby

Lombok Strait
Feb. 18–19 1942

1943

1943

AUSTRALIA

RIGHT: **The first wave of attacking US Marines in LVTs heading to the beach at Iwo Jima as the first part of Operation "Detachment" on February 15, 1945. The smoke from naval support gunfire is lifting to reveal the objective. Mount Suribachi is clearly visible.**

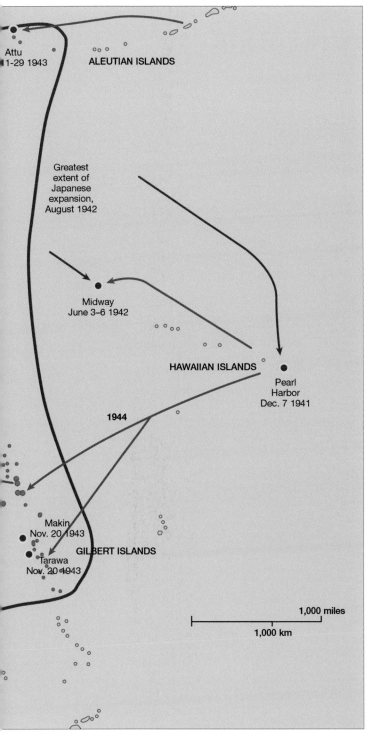

The Pacific campaign

The surprise attack on the US Naval base at Pearl Harbor on December 7, 1941 was the beginning of Japan's rapid expansion into the Pacific. An invasion of the Philippines and Guam (December 10, 1941) and then the landings on the Burma mainland (December 11, 1941) were followed by actions to capture Borneo, Luzon, Hong Kong and Manila (January 2, 1942). By April 9, 1942, the last US troops had surrendered at Mindanao.

In May 1942, the Japanese Imperial Navy was again defeated at the Battle of the Coral Sea off New Guinea. What is said to have been the turning point of the war in the Pacific was the Battle of Midway (June 4/5, 1942), a decisive victory for US naval airpower. On August 7, 1942, the first amphibious landing of the war by US forces was launched against the Japanese on Guadacanal and Tulagi in the Solomons. The enemy ceased fire on February 9, 1943.

In 1943, the US military kept pressure on Japanese forces with amphibious assaults against targets, including the Aleutian Islands, Lae-Salamaua, Bougainville and Makin/Tarawa. The last actions of the year were the Allied (US, NZ and Australian) landings on New Britain.

The first landing of 1944 was against Kwajalein on January 31, which was captured by February 7. Further attacks were carried out during the year against other targets, which included the islands of Saipan (June 15), Guam (July 19) and Leyte (October 20). US forces landed on Mindoro (Philippines) on December 15, 1944.

On January 9, 1945, US forces attacked Luzon. By now, Japanese resistance had become resolute as enemy forces approached closer to the mainland. The assault on Iwo Jima (February 15, 1945) saw heavy fighting and many casualties on both sides. On April 1, 1945, the last amphibious landing of the war took place against Okinawa. After almost two months of bloody fighting, Japanese forces finally surrendered to the US Tenth Army on June 22, 1945.

The first atomic bomb (A-Bomb) "Little Boy" was dropped on Hiroshima on August 6, 1945, with devastating results. A second A-Bomb "Fat Man" was dropped on August 9, 1945, the target being Nagasaki.

On August 14, 1945, Japan accepted an unconditional surrender. The requirement for the planned amphibious assault on Japan was forgotten.

ABOVE LEFT: **This map shows Allied advances in the Pacific theatre from 1943–45. During this time, US military planners began the task of assembling a force to retake the island groups captured by the Japanese. The plan was to use a powerful amphibious force supported by warships to capture an island group, then use this as a base for the assault on the next group.**

LEFT: **The massive firepower of US Navy battleships was used to great effect for the pre-landing barrage. The ships also supplied support fire when requested by troops on the ground. This is USS *Nevada* (BB-36).**

Operation "Toenails", New Georgia and Rendova

With the Japanese evacuation of Guadalcanal in February 1943, US forces sought to maintain momentum, moving in stages up the Solomons chain toward the enemy stronghold of Rabaul. The chosen method was to take only strategically significant islands, bypassing others, leaving the occupying Japanese garrisons to await their fate.

For both sides, airfields were vital, and governed the length of any advance. Less than 322km/200 miles from Henderson Field on Guadalcanal was the Japanese airstrip at Munda, on the island of New Georgia. This, with a small strip on neighbouring Kolombangara, was used as a staging post for Japanese air strikes on Guadalcanal. To the US military, the capture of Munda would be strategically vital.

Thinly spread over their vast conquests, the Japanese could not be everywhere. The native islanders detested them, in general remaining loyal to their, usually, Australian District Officers. Most of these had stayed on, leading a fugitive existence as "Coastwatchers" and provided an invaluable intelligence network as well as giving early warning of Japanese air raids coming down "The Slot", the channel running the length of the Solomons.

A division of Vice-Admiral William F. Halsey's US 3rd Fleet, the amphibious force of Rear-Admiral Richmond K. ("Terrible") Turner had been expanded considerably. He now controlled seven transport divisions, comprising Transports (APA), Cargo Ships (AK) and Fast Destroyer Transports (APD). Eighteen LSTs and 48 LCTs were also organized in divisions. Finally, there were the Coastal Transports (APC) and five Fast Destroyer Minesweepers (DMS).

ABOVE: **US troops clambering down landing nets to waiting landing craft at Empress Augustus Bay after the islands had been recaptured.**
LEFT: **The assault force was landed at the very edge of the jungle, which concealed Japanese troops in camouflaged positions.**

ABOVE: **US Marines using a bulldozer to haul a trailer loaded with supplies through the thick mud common to Bougainville Island.** LEFT: **The Japanese airfield of Munda on New Georgia under attack by US aircraft.**

Although on New Georgia the Japanese presence was concentrated around the Munda airfield, reports indicated small detachments at four other points. The US military reasoned that, if these were vital enough to interest the enemy, they were worth capturing.

As frontal assault on reef-fringed Munda would have been unnecessarily costly, the main landing was aimed at the northern end of the neighbouring island of Rendova. A natural harbour was here only 8km/5 miles across the strait from Munda and was backed by high ground reaching to over 914m/3,000ft, allowing Munda to be commanded both by observation and artillery. Five landings were conducted simultaneously on June 30, 1943. The four on New Georgia – at Viru Harbour, Segi Point, Wickham Anchorage and Onaiavisi – were minor actions, involving only APDs, LCTs and LCIs.

For Rendova, a first echelon of 6,300 troops was brought in by four APA and two AKs, with Turner flying his flag in USS *McCawley* (APA-4), known irreverently as the "Wacky Mac". Three further echelons made scheduled landings in APDs and LSTs. The initial ship-to-shore operation was "nearly perfect", all troops being ashore within 30 yards of the first wave. Within two hours, Munda was being shelled by US forces using 105mm howitzers.

Although the operations had been "soft", the Japanese reacted strongly with air attacks. Despite US fighter cover from Guadalcanal and the neighbouring Russells, the large ships were heavily attacked as they withdrew from Rendova. USS *McCawley* (APA-4) had off-loaded 1,100 troops, over 600 tons of equipment along with senior Army and Navy officers. The ship was, therefore, empty when torpedoed in the machinery space. Severely damaged and settling, the ship was taken in tow. After nightfall, almost unbelievably, USS *McCawley* was torpedoed and sunk in error by the US Navy PT boats.

The secondary landings had yielded no more than anchorages and inlets of use to minor warships. Although positions on Rendova rendered the Munda airstrip virtually unusable, this did not prevent the Japanese turning New Georgia into a latter-day Guadalcanal. Recent history was repeated as both sides built up their presence, the Japanese by a reinstatement of their "Tokyo Express". As vicious jungle fighting progressed ashore, fierce night skirmishes occurred offshore. These ranged from PT boats intercepting Japanese barge traffic to the fierce and damaging warship battles in Kula Gulf and Kolombangara. Only in August 1943 was New Georgia finally captured.

BELOW: **General MacArthur's policy of "hitting 'em where they ain't" resulted in many landings by US Marines being unopposed by Japanese forces.**

Operation "Postern", Lae/Salamaua, New Guinea

Complementing Admiral Nimitz's drive across the Central Pacific was General Douglas MacArthur's southern campaign, aimed at threatening Japan via New Guinea, the Philippines, Formosa and China. Although this would always be the secondary threat, the Japanese could never afford to take it less than seriously.

Although conceited, MacArthur was nonetheless a master of manoeuvre warfare. Compared with Nimitz, he was always short of resources, always out-numbered. He compensated by outsmarting the enemy, encouraging them, via superior codebreaking, to believe that he would do what was expected, before doing something entirely different. He resisted being drawn into attritional jungle warfare but unbalanced the numerically superior enemy by seemingly opportunist moves, before quickly moving on. In a word, he maintained the tempo of an operation while, in the much-quoted phrase "hitting 'em where they ain't".

Japanese forces were concentrated on the north coast of New Guinea, among the main centres of population. This facilitated logistics and back-up by the Imperial Japanese Navy, but made them vulnerable to the amphibious, coast-hopping style of warfare practised by "MacArthur's Navy". No advance could safely be conducted beyond the maximum 321km/200 miles range of land-based air support. Just, however, as this influenced Japanese assessment of his next likely move, MacArthur would use Nimitz's fleet carriers to cover a more ambitious push forward, wrong-footing the enemy yet again. Airstrips would be rapidly constructed, releasing the carriers.

RIGHT: **US and Australian forces cooperated closely during the long New Guinea campaign. The US-built LCM(3) could accommodate a 30-ton tank. A Matilda medium tank of the Australian Army is being unloaded here.**

RIGHT: **For the most part, the Allies enjoyed air superiority, which permitted the under-strength "MacArthur's Navy" to take chances, as here, where seven LSTs are openly beached in line, an inviting target for attacking aircraft.**

ABOVE: **A Landing Ship, Tank (LST) loaded with Australian forces heads to the beachhead.** LEFT: **New Guinea was an infantryman's war, one of jungle-clad mountains and muddy tracks. The Japanese were dug in on the northern coastal strip.**

With US troops now across their lines of communication, the Japanese would either have to accept battle on MacArthur's terms, or as was often the case, embark on desperate jungle treks in order to rejoin the main force.

The huge island of Papua New Guinea is shaped like an ungainly bird, facing westward. Around 483km/300 miles from its "tail" lies the Huon Gulf, upon which is situated the settlement of Lae, with a useful, deep-water port and airfield. Strongly held by the Japanese, Lae had views across the gulf to Salamaua, some 40km/25 miles distant.

MacArthur wanted Lae, and his strategy was simple. During July 1943 his motor torpedo boats set up a blockade of the gulf, disrupting the endless convoy of supply craft upon which the Japanese garrison depended. He then moved a mainly Australian force from the interior in the direction of Salamaua in order to construct a dummy airstrip. A token US force was then moved up the coast.

To the Japanese, all the signs pointed to an imminent assault on Salamaua, and they moved 80 per cent of their strength from Lae as cover. The Allied force, having fooled the enemy, thus avoided battle while remaining the focus of Japanese interest. Only 2,000 Japanese remained around Lae, and little opposition greeted the 9th Australian Division on September 4, as preceded by a destroyer bombardment, a landing was made 19km/12 miles to the east by the Amphibious Force ("VII Phib") of the 7th Fleet, under its capable commander, Rear-Admiral Daniel E. Barbey ("Uncle Dan the Amphibious Man").

Unable to retrace its steps quickly enough through the deep jungle mud, the greater Japanese force attacking Salamaua was helpless to intervene. This allowed Barbey's landing craft to speed to the landing site despite air attacks.

As the Australian troops closed on Lae from the east, 1,700 US paratroops were dropped to the west. The airstrip was quickly secured allowing further ground troops to be flown in. Declining battle with the now considerably larger Allied force, the Lae garrison withdrew, leaving the town by September 16.

The Japanese at Salamaua were now neatly contained and, with no hope of reinforcement or evacuation by sea they, also, escaped to the jungle on treks that resulted in the death of a very high proportion through disease, malnutrition or exhaustion.

LEFT: **Australian forces unloading fuel, vehicles and other supplies from LSTs of the US Navy.**

ABOVE: **Men of the 2nd Marine Division begin the break-out from the landing beach.** LEFT: **The deceptive calm of the transport anchorage while loaded LCVs prepare for the assault phase. Note the LVT being put afloat from the transport *Doyen* (AP-2) by cargo derrick.**

Operation "Galvanic", Makin and Tarawa, Gilbert Islands

Around 2,253km/1,400 miles to the northeast of the still-disputed Solomons, and threatening their flank, lay the 16 scattered atolls of the Gilbert Islands, The Japanese occupied only two in force; Butaritari on Makin harboured a seaplane base and Betio on Tarawa an airfield. Admiral Nimitz wanted both islands as a staging point for an imminent advance on the neighbouring Marshall Islands.

As early as August 1942, a US forces raid on Makin had alerted the Japanese to US military interest, and both islands were systematically fortified, theoretically to allow the defenders to resist until relieved in three to seven days.

Planning for Operation "Galvanic" emphasized speed of execution, for the US Navy did not want to risk aircraft carriers a moment longer than necessary. The USMC had already witnessed this policy at Guadalcanal and had lost some trust in the commitment of the US Navy.

This would be the first strongly opposed assault. Both islands were ringed by shallow lagoons skirted by wide and barely submerged reefs. Tidal ranges were small and barely surveyed. Landing craft, LCMs and LCVPs, would be likely to ground due to the shallow water, so 125 LVTs were allocated to transport the initial three assault waves at Tarawa. Another 50 LVTs were to be on the assault at Makin.

Of the US 5th Fleet's Amphibious Corps, the 2nd Marine Division was allocated Tarawa. The less-experienced US Army 27th Infantry Division was sent to Makin. Total US strength was 27,600; enemy strength was an estimated 5,400, all being very well prepared.

For days before, aircraft from Vice-Admiral Spruance's 5th Fleet carriers had attacked a range of enemy-held islands, both to disguise the true objective and to reduce Japanese resources in aircraft and ammunition.

ABOVE: **Many of the 14 Japanese coast defence guns on Betio were of British manufacture and captured earlier at Singapore.** LEFT: **One of the many blockhouse-type defensive strongpoints built by the Japanese.**

ABOVE: **Firmly ashore but by no means yet secure, these US Marines are having to clear the mass of equipment blocking the narrow beach.** LEFT: **The hulks of abandoned LVTs bear silent witness to the ferocity of the defences at Betio.**

Both assaults were timed for early on November 20, 1943. That on Butaritari (Makin) initially met light opposition; fortunately, for with only 50 LVTs most of the 6,500 US troops had to wade 300 yards across the waist-deep lagoon. Less than 20 per cent of the planned backup LCM/LCVP supply journeys made it over the reef on the first day.

Fighting literally to the last man, the Japanese held out for four days. Far longer than scheduled, this delay vindicated the US Navy's caution when an escort carrier was torpedoed by a Japanese submarine and sank with only a few survivors.

Betio was "the real toughie". Just 3.2km/2 miles in length and of an area estimated at under 120 hectares/300 acres, it was a fortress. A solid barrier of coconut logs ringed the shoreline. There were 14 coastal gun and 25 field gun emplacements, dug-in tanks with 37mm guns, and innumerable covered and armoured machine-gun positions. There were also deep, fortified bunkers. Mined reefs and beach obstacles guided landing craft into the chosen field of artillery fire. Combined with carrier-borne air attacks, bombardment ships laid some 3,000 tons of ordnance on the defenders

over the two hours that preceded the first landing. It would prove to be "woefully inadequate". Inaccurate marking of the Line of Departure and unfavourable sea conditions saw the first waves of LVTs arrive 43 minutes late. As the support bombardment had ceased on schedule, this lapse gave the defenders adequate time to re-man their positions.

In negotiating the reef and lagoon, the lightly armoured LVTs and the troops thus took a terrible beating. With survivors trying to regroup under the cover of the log barrier, the follow-up troops were stranded on the reef as their assault craft grounded in the shallow water.

The assault stalled. Of the 125 LVTs launched 90 were disabled, the remainder being used to ferry the wounded to landing craft and returning with fresh troops, just 25 at a time.

Gradual reinforcement and raw courage saw the invaders slowly gain the initiative. Seventy-six hours later Betio was again silent. Over 1,000 US soldiers had died, and 4,700 Japanese were dead, just 19 were captured. Appalled at the carnage the USMC commander, Major General Holland M. ("Howlin' Mad") Smith was moved to write that "Tarawa was a mistake".

LEFT: **US forces were firmly established on Tarawa on December 31, 1943. The newly constructed airfield can be seen in the background, but off the beach there remain the hulks of LVTs and landing craft sunk during the landing.**

LEFT: **The twin island of Roi-Namur, the major objective on the Kwajalein Atoll, absorbed over 7,400 rounds of ordnance fired by ships of the US Navy in the 48 hours preceding the assault. Through unexpectedly rough conditions, the first two waves of LVTs are approaching the smoke-shrouded shore.**

Operation "Flintlock", Kwajalien, Marshall Islands

Lying to the north of the Gilberts, the Marshall Islands were the first of the groups mandated to Japan following World War I to be attacked. Having been closed to foreigners, suspicions grew that, despite the conditions of the Washington Treaty, the islands had been well fortified. The bloody seizure of the Gilberts, besides giving valuable experience in opposed landings, provided the necessary base for reconnaissance and eventual occupation of the Marshalls.

Stung by the criticism of inadequate fire support at Tarawa, the US 5th Fleet would more than compensate at the Marshalls. That Tarawa had been a success at all had been due to the use of LVTs. However, such was the attrition rate that 300 were now considered the minimum for a division-strength landing. Deep bunkers and fortified emplacements on Tarawa showed the need for great numbers of flamethrowers, satchel charges and bazookas. Specialist underwater teams would be required to clear obstacles and mines.

A total of 26,500 Japanese troops were spread among the 34 atolls of the islands, where six airfields, four seaplane bases and three naval anchorages had been established. Resources permitted only one atoll to be hit at a time and Nitmitz decided on Kwajalein. Here, major assaults would be staged on the two

ABOVE: **US troops and supplies being landed from an LST on Kwajalien Atoll on April 15, 1944, after the last Japanese had been defeated.**

islands, Kwajalein and Roi-Namur. The US Army 7th Infantry Division was allocated Kwajalein, where there was a 5,000-strong garrison. Roi-Namur, with 3,000 Japanese defenders, was allocated to the untried 4th Marine Division.

The strategy carried some risk (and attracted criticism) in that it would bypass several powerful enemy garrisons who, if unwilling to simply await their fate, would need to be neutralized later. For the moment, aircraft from Spruance's carriers swept the Marshall Islands clear of Japanese aircraft and completed essential photographic intelligence.

Prior to the assault on January 31, 1944, the island of Roi-Namur was subjected to a 48-hour naval bombardment which, later, was estimated to have killed or incapacitated over half of the defenders.

Overseen by senior officers on board USS *Appalachian* (AGC-1) the first, purpose-built Headquarters Ship, troops disembarked from transport ships to LCVPs. Those slated for the first wave then transferred to 244 LVTs, floated from new LSDs and LSTs. In rough conditions they were marshalled into approximately straight lines. Each wave was directly supported by rocket-firing LCIs (known as "Elsie Items") and some of the 75 available armoured LVTs, with 37mm guns, which could land and function as light tanks.

Small flanking islands had been seized earlier for the establishment of artillery. While they worked well, these subsidiary landings broke up the LVT and landing craft fleet, which never fully recovered formation.

Still shocked by the bombardment, the surviving Japanese fought courageously but within 48 hours, Roi-Namur, "a stinking mess of debris and dead Japanese" was subdued.

At Kwajalein, the landing was supported by three carriers, three battleships, a cruiser and nine destroyers. The bombardment used up approximately 1,000 x 16in,

ABOVE **On Einwetok, as ever, Japanese defenders fought to the end. Only 64 were taken prisoner, and some 2,700 died.**

1,340 x 14in, 400 x 8in and 5,000 x 5in rounds of ammunition. Neighbouring islets were again seized for the establishment of artillery batteries.

The first four waves of LVTs, supported by armoured LVTs and rocket-firing LCIs hit the beach within the space of 12 minutes. Follow-up landing craft experienced trouble, grounding on isolated coral reefs.

The island, which was 3.2km/2 miles in length, had been reduced to craters and tangled rubble in which small groups of Japanese troops were fought in vicious hand-to-hand combat. It took four days for US troops to fight their way from one end of the island to the other.

It would take until the April to clear pockets of enemy resistance throughout the Marshalls but, by then, the war had moved on. Boeing B-29 Superfortress aircraft were rapidly deployed to start bombing the Marianas, Nimitz's next objective.

LEFT: **An LCM from USS *Sumter* (APA-52), a war-built attack transport, being unloaded by SeeBees equipped with a bulldozer.**

57

Operation "Overlord", Normandy

The Normandy landing was on a scale that made earlier operations appear to have been rehearsal, and much depended on the success of the operation. Despite fighting on major fronts in the east and in Italy, Germany had gathered a massive military force in northern France. The Allied re-entry into "Fortress Europe" had long been anticipated. Mounted from England, the extent would be such that the only suitable locations were the beaches of either the Pas de Calais or Normandy. Deception was thus vital to the Allied cause, for any German guess had a 50 per cent chance of being correct.

Germany's best-qualified field officers commanded in France, Field Marshal Gerd von Rundstedt had overall regional control as C-in-C, while Field Marshal Erwin Rommel was responsible for Army Group B, whose 7th Army garrisoned the western Channel coast. The two agreed to differ over defensive strategy, the infantry divisions being entrenched within the extensive fortifications of the vaunted "Atlantic Wall", with the armoured divisions held back as the mobile reserve, to be rushed to whichever location the Allies committed to attack.

To move armour rapidly the *Wehrmacht* required road and rail links and, for months before, Allied tactical air forces had specifically targeted what appeared to be strategically significant bridges and junctions in random air-raiding patterns that indicated no particular preference.

Allied planners knew that success would hinge on a race for reinforcement. Once a beachhead was secured, resources would have to be poured in at a faster rate than the enemy could reinforce his defences. The Dieppe experience of 1942 had convinced planners that an assault on or near a major port would be doomed to failure. Thus, "Mulberry" was conceived: two complete port facilities made up of floatable concrete modules were to be towed across the Channel, positioned and sunk on site. These would allow large ships to discharge vehicles directly just 850 yards from the beach. Vehicle access would be via floating causeways.

Considerable pressure had been exerted by both the Soviet Union and United States to mount the assault even as early as 1942. The British had resisted strongly until the necessary resources and combat skills were available. Also, air and sea superiority had to be firmly established by Allied forces.

By 1944 the *Luftwaffe* was much reduced, with the best units withdrawn back to defend the "Fatherland" against the onslaught of the US and British heavy bomber forces.

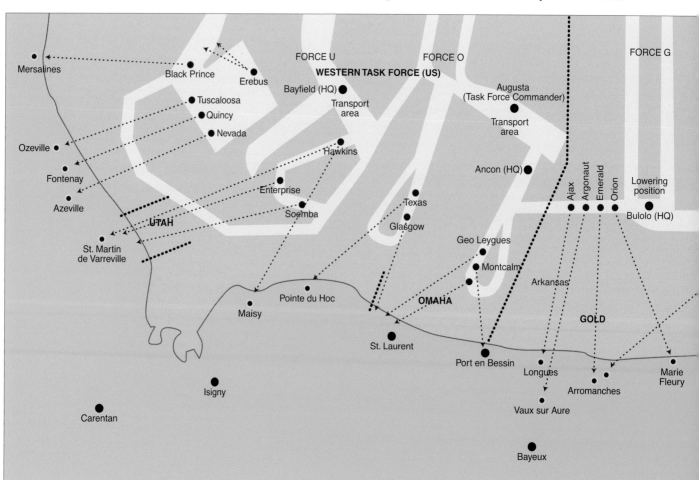

ABOVE: **No less than 33 LCIs were included in the V Corps assault convoy. The vessels are flying barrage balloons to discourage low-level air attack.**
RIGHT: **On D-Day a vast number of different types of vessel were used.**

A bonus of the now-established Allied air superiority over the English Channel was that *Luftwaffe* reconnaissance flights were rare. Unable to confirm any suspicions, the Germans were more susceptible to skilful deception. In south-east England, for instance, a wholly fictitious "American First Army Group" was created, with signal traffic so realistic that, for weeks following "Overlord", powerful elements of the German 15th Army were held back in readiness for a further landing in the Pas de Calais.

BELOW: **A schematic plan of the amphibious landings on D-Day, June 6, 1944. The beaches were codenamed "Utah" (US), "Omaha" (US), "Gold" (British), "Juno" (Canadian) and "Sword" (British).**

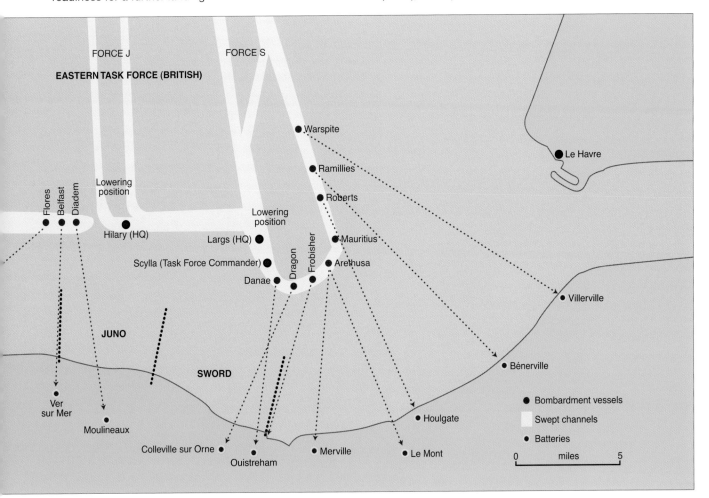

LEFT: **The view aboard an LCT prior to the Normandy landings. In the foreground is a Sherman M4A-1 tank fitted with deep water wading trunking, one for the exhaust the other for air to the engine.**

To create a beachhead of a size to base forces sufficient to contain known German strength, a five-division front was required. Five beach sectors were thus created, stretching some 96km/60 miles from the Orne estuary to a point on the Cotentin peninsula. In the east, the British beaches, "Gold" and "Sword", bracketed the Canadian "Juno". The long US forces "Omaha" beach then joined "Utah" in the far west.

Six hours ahead of the main assault, two airborne divisions would seize vital bridgeheads. The invading force was due to be built up at the rate of one and one-third divisions each day.

The maritime side of the operation was so large as to merit its own organization. Operation "Neptune" was headed by Admiral Sir Bertram Ramsay who, four years earlier, had overseen the Dunkirk evacuation. The two western (US) beaches, conduit for the US First Army, were the responsibility of the Western Task Force, under Rear-Admiral Alan G. Kirk. The British Second Army was to be passed through the three eastern beach sectors, controlled by Rear-Admiral Sir Philip Vian's Eastern Task Force. Until landed, all military forces were subordinate to the navy.

RIGHT: **A Dodge WC-54 ambulance being loaded on to an LST at Weymouth in Dorset prior to the D-Day landings. A damaged drive unit from a landing craft has been dumped on the quayside.**

By stripping every command of all possible vessels, the Royal Navy supplied the greater part of the 1,213 warships participating. As the average crossing was under 161km/100 miles, smaller assault craft could, weather permitting, make the passage. Complex vessels such as LSDs were thus little used. Among the craft assembled were 236 LSTs, 837 LCTs and 248 LCIs. British forces landed from LCAs, of which there were over 500. US troops landed from LCVPs, some 190 in total.

British ports and estuaries from Milford Haven, Wales to Great Yarmouth, Norfolk were full of shipping during the preparation phase. The coastal convoy system was heavily utilized. Experienced escort groups and Coastal Command squadrons were tasked with making the Channel inaccessible to U-boats. Air cover could be based on English airfields, greatly increasing aircraft utilization and pilot survival.

ABOVE: **Men of No. 47 (Royal Marine) Commando landing from LCAs on "Gold" beach, June 6, 1944. No. 47 Commando was tasked to capture Port-en-Bessin and then join US forces who had landed at "Omaha" beach.**

The Germans had confidence in the abilities of the "Oyster" pressure mine, familiar to the Allies and deemed unsweepable. Not for the first time in history, however, was a weapon thought so secret and important that it could not be used before the event. Again, the outcome was that huge stockpiles had been accumulated but, at the last minute, there was no opportunity to lay them. Subsequent night drops by the *Luftwaffe* and E-boats would demonstrate how large a nuisance these could have been. After some five years of war, the relatively shallow waters of the Channel were infested with mines of all types.

ABOVE: **US Rangers in British LCAs being loaded aboard HMS *Prince Baudouin*, a fast troop transport, prior to landing on "Omaha" beach.**

ABOVE: **British troops of the 50th (Northumbrian) Division move to "Gold" beach in LCVs. A transport ship burns after an air attack.**

LEFT: **Approaching touchdown, the troops in this LCV must have been relieved to see the personnel on the beach and apparent lack of opposition. Despite initial firece fighting, even on "Omaha" beach direct opposition was quelled relatively quickly.**

A cleared assembly area was thus created south of the Isle of Wight, served by four swept channels connecting with the coastal convoy route. From this area, eight parallel swept channels ran southward to the known German minefields, which ran parallel to the French coast. On D-Day, Fleet Minesweepers would work ahead of the armada to clear ten safe routes through the minefields before creating safe manoeuvring areas for fire support ships.

Because of the density of beach obstructions, landing had to be fixed for three to four hours before high water. To make it just before first light, the date was set for June 5, 1944, but poor weather enforced an anxious 24-hour delay. As it was, many beach obstacles were submerged.

Because of tidal differences along the length of the Normandy coast, "H-hour" on the two US beaches was at 06:30, one hour ahead of the remainder. More beach obstacles were exposed and could be avoided, but on "Omaha" the sheer width of beach was a drawback. The Germans had fortified the low bluffs that overlooked the sands, and exits were limited and well covered. Despite advice from his own senior US Marine Corps officers, Rear-Admiral Kirk limited the preliminary bombardment to only 40 minutes in order to maintain surprise for as long as possible. It proved to be painfully insufficient.

Tidal conditions enforced a delay on "Sword" but this was utilized for further heavy naval bombardment. Poor visibility caused by smoke and dust hampered air spotting. With the landings in progress, destroyers continually patroled close-in to attack requested targets and give visible support. During the critical opening phase these vessels gave a tremendous boost to the morale of those troops ashore.

Initial waves were supported by amphibious "DD" tanks. Once ashore, these were invaluable but, in the conditions, many were launched too far out and either came ashore in the wrong location or sank in the choppy seas. Following closely were the first LCTs, carrying tanks modified for beach clearance, which complemented explosive devices to establish safe paths through the minefields. Before D-Day was over, 132,000 Allied troops were ashore at the cost of just over 10,000 casualties. The race was on for reinforcement and resupply. It was won by the Allies thanks to meticulous planning and greater resources.

ABOVE: **"Omaha" beach two days after D-Day, in which US reinforcements, including heavy artillery, were moving inland. DUKW amphibious vehicles were being utilized to carry supplies from transport ships.** LEFT: **Deceptively peaceful, this view from Arromanches shows the "Mulberry" harbour, "Gooseberry", the floating causeways and the "Lobnitz" pierheads.**

Operation "Infatuate II", Walcheren

By October 1944, the port of Antwerp, the facilities of which were desperately needed to support the Allied advance into Germany, was in British hands. Situated some 81km/50 miles up the Scheldt estuary, however, it remained unusable as the river was mined. In addition, the Germans, aware of the strategic importance of the port, still held the seaward end. The mainland, and the south bank around Breskens, was in Allied hands by October 31 but the north side, the island of Walcheren, remained heavily defended by the Germans.

Walcheren is some 13km/8 miles across. Only the coastal rim and the major towns lay above sea level. A first move, reluctantly, was to breach the sea dykes by bombing, flooding the interior and leaving the formidable German defences marooned on a narrow strip of land. Some 60 guns, of calibres from 2cm to 75cm, located in concrete emplacements around Westkapelle, were linked as a continuous line of defence.

Learning from the Dieppe experience, heavy support fire was supplied for the assault. In the event, the effect of the 15in shells fired from a battleship and two monitors from a range of 21km/13 miles was largely wasted as the weather was too cloudy to allow aerial spotting.

ABOVE: **As the smoke screen disperses, Royal Marine commandos are moving ashore in DUKWs. LCT 952 is positioned ready to land vehicles.**

ABOVE: **Commandos and equipment were transported in 35 LCTs. These personnel were embarked with "Buffalos", the British name for the LVT.**
LEFT: **On the left flank of the assault, the Westkapelle sea dyke was breached by RAF bombing, flooding the inland area.**

Fortunately, a 25-strong Support Squadron had been formed, comprising LCG (L), LCG (M), LCF and LCT (R), the approaches being too shallow for warships. A further innovation was US-supplied LVTs, known to the British as "Buffalos" and able to transport 24 equipped troops. There had, however, been no time to exercise with them.

Four hours after an assault was to be mounted across the river from Breskens, three Royal Marine Commando (Nos. 41, 47 and 48) were to be landed to straddle the gap in the sea dyke by Westkapelle.

A total of 181 craft of all types assembled off Ostend early on November 1. The weather at dawn was calm and heavily overcast as the force approached the Dutch coast. Landing was timed for 09:45, following naval gunfire and aerial bombardment, which was greatly reduced in effect by the overcast weather.

LEFT: **Indispensable on sand, perhaps even more so in the mud of Holland, tracked vehicles such as the "Weasel" and "Buffalo" were able to negotiate the foreshore and drive over the sea wall.**

LEFT: **A Sherman Crab flail tank landing from an LCT to clear mines. The type was one of those special vehicles developed by Major Percy Hobart of the 79th Armoured Division.**

It has been stated that this would be the most heavily opposed landing of World War II, and certainly the gun batteries and strongpoints, which had withheld fire down to approximately 3,000 yards, appeared to form a continuous line. Under a murderous barrage, the 25 craft of the Support Squadron engaged the enemy at near-suicidal ranges. All were damaged, some deliberately being beached to form unsinkable, stationary strongpoints. The battle, which lasted over three hours, drew the highest praise, but the price was considerable. Nine craft were sunk and eleven damaged, seven of them seriously. Personnel losses were 170 dead and 125 injured.

The dedication of the Support Squadron was not wasted. Many LVTs were floated from LCTs offshore and came ashore in company with the LCI (S). Once ashore, many were below trajectory of the large enemy guns, which could not be depressed sufficiently. Delayed by beach congestion, the LCTs of No. 47 Commando were shelled when ordered in, but were beached satisfactorily.

Established on either side of the gap, increasingly supported from the air, the commandos began to clear the enemy defences. German marines resisted resolutely, infantry less so, and prisoners began to be taken in embarrassingly large numbers. Despite great difficulties in resupply, progress was steady, Walcheren being cleared in eight days; the cost to the commandos was 79 dead. Minesweepers quickly cleared the Scheldt, and massive quantities of supplies were passing through Antwerp by the end of November.

The assault on Walcheren, the last such in the European theatre during World War II, was successful largely because the German batteries fired on the Support Squadron rather than engaging the assault craft during the vulnerable approach phase. Although successful in the Pacific, the LVTs were difficult to handle in the river currents. Once ashore, the LVT was liable to sink in soft sand and mud, and it could not negotiate steep sand dunes. The "Buffalo" did, however, save many lives.

ABOVE: **Landing Craft, Gun (Medium) 101, sinking after being hit several times by shells from a German coastal battery.**

Operation "Forager", Saipan, Marianas

The southern Mariana Islands were around 1,609km/ 1,000 miles from the US forces' forward base in the Marshalls, and any assault on them would need to be self-supporting, with carrier-based air support. Regarded by the Japanese as part of their home territory, the Marianas would be defended to the last. In US hands the Carolines to the south would cut off and provide flank cover for MacArthur's southern campaign. They would also provide the necessary air and naval bases for the staging of strikes directly at the enemy's home islands.

Staged in the same month as the Normandy landings, Operation "Forager" had to compete for resources, yet mustered 535 ships and craft and a total of 165,000 troops.

The southern Marianas, specifically Saipan, Tinian and Guam, lay in a 161km/100-mile straight line. Coral-fringed, all were rugged, relatively large and well-populated. Saipan, the most northerly, is just 2,092km/1,300 miles from Tokyo. Taken first, it would isolate Tinian and Guam from reinforcement.

Against Saipan and the smaller Tinian was ranged the Northern Attack Force, carrying General Holland M. Smith's "V Phib Corps". This comprised the reinforced 2nd and 4th

ABOVE: **Submarines of the US Navy played a vital role in the Pacific theatre by attacking Japanese transport shipping and warships.**

USMC divisions. A separate Southern Attack Force was allocated to Guam. Two further Army divisions were held in reserve. Saipan was to be attacked first, on June 15, 1944, with attacks on Tinian and Guam following at a date which depended on progress after the initial landing.

The invasion forces left from Hawaii and Guadalcanal, respectively 5,633km/3,500 miles and 3,862km/2,400 miles from the objectives. Shielding the force from a vengeful

LEFT: **Transport anchorages needed to be established at a distance from the shore, yet not so far as to hazard LCVPs and LVTs. This photograph shows USS *Sumter* (APA-52) (right) and USS *Almaack* (AKA-10) loaded with ammunition, attached to Transdiv 26, at anchor off Tinian.**

LEFT: **An LVT (4), loaded with US Marines, headed for Tinian. The "turret" mounted two 0.30in machine-guns. A single 0.50in heavy machine-gun is mounted in the rear of the cargo bay.**

LEFT: **The beachhead is now established, allowing a constant stream of LCVPs to bring ashore vehicles, stores and personnel. Note, a slipway has been built and covered with metal road matting.** BELOW: **US Marines were pinned down by Japanese forces who had pre-targeted the beach.**

Imperial Japanese Navy was Spruance's powerful 5th Fleet. Even as Saipan was attacked, Admiral Ozawa's battle fleet sailed for the Marianas. The resulting confrontation with Spruance, the Battle of the Philippine Sea, was one of the great aircraft carrier battles of World War II.

Saipan was defended in depth by nearly 32,000 Japanese Army and Navy personnel. There would have been more, but US submarines had intercepted most of the transports carrying reinforcements to the island.

Two hours of naval bombardment commenced at 04:30 on June 15. This was followed by 30 minutes of air strikes, then further bombardment until touchdown at 08:44. A large secondary landing was, meanwhile, in progress some 16km/10 miles to the north.

The two divisions were landed on a continuous 6,000-yard beachhead divided into eight equal sectors. In each sector, four assault waves would touch down within 21 minutes, putting the first 8,000 troops ashore. Each assault wave comprised 12 LVTs, covered by 18 armoured and gun-armed LVTs. Landing Craft, Control (LCC) flanked the lines of LVTs. Leading in each sector were three rocket-firing LCIs. Once the troops had landed, each LVT was driven through the incoming waves of LVTs to the transports and reloaded with fresh troops.

Fronted by a reef of up to 700 yards in width, the beaches fringed a flat and bare sandy plain nearly 1.6km/1 mile wide. Japanese artillery had pre-targeted every salient point and was too-well dispersed to have been neutralized by the pre-landing bombardment. As at Salerno, this destroyed anything that moved. US forces were pinned to the narrow beachheads, and objectives for Day 1 were not taken until Day 3.

LSTs followed-up the assault landing, unloading further LVTs and DUKWs on to the reef. Two LSDs off-loaded LCMs pre-loaded with 36 tanks. Despite this armour, destroyers still had to sail close to the reef in order to attack Japanese tank columns while under direct fire. Heavier fire support ships had been diverted to meet the urgent threat posed by the Japanese fleet, shortly to be engaged by Spruance.

By Day 3, the foothold was reasonably secure, with 50,000 troops and ample artillery ashore, but the whole island would require a further three weeks to conquer. It would be a tough assignment. Out of the 67,000 US troops eventually involved, over 16,500 were casualties, with more than 3,400 dead or missing. Over 24,000 Japanese died. The losses in US resources delayed the landings on Guam by a month.

ABOVE: **US Marines provide covering machine-gun fire as infantry supported by Sherman tanks advance on enemy positions.**

67

ABOVE: **The Japanese airfield, which was the main target on Hollandia, after attack by US Navy dive-bombers.** LEFT: **Australian troops waiting to load on board an LST as part of the second wave attack force for Lae.**

New Guinea

The combination of General MacArthur's particular talents and the topography of New Guinea produced a mode of amphibious warfare entirely different to that imposed upon Admiral Nimitz for the Central Pacific Theatre.

The 2,253km/1,400 mile north coast of New Guinea is backed by vast tracts of mountain and virgin equatorial jungle. As with the previous colonial administrators, the Japanese "occupied" or "controlled" the island only by virtue of holding a string of coastal settlements. With no defence in depth, the region was quickly captured by the Japanese in 1942, but now this flaw exposed the Japanese occupiers to the same hazard of rapid defeat.

MacArthur did not have the resources, time nor inclination to give the enemy an advantage by advancing along the length of the coastline. He employed instead a series of amphibious bypassing operations, in which prior intelligence and deception were to play a major role.

By the end of 1943 the Japanese were thinking defensively, basing their defensive positions upon the appreciation of where US forces would strike next. As exemplified at Lae/Salamana in September 1943, General MacArthur, fully aware by code-breaking and POW interrogation, effectively fooled the main Japanese force, by apparently doing what they expected him to do, before landing, nearly unopposed, in their rear.

In Rear-Admiral Daniel E. Barbey's "VII Phib", MacArthur had the (albeit ever-inadequate) mobility resource, but the key to his success lay in his establishment of joint-service headquarters, planning and command organization, promoting maximum flexibility through harmonious inter-service relationships at every level. This encouraged a tempo of operations that the Japanese

BELOW LEFT: **Landing craft and support vessels unloading supplies for the invasion force on Tanahmera Bay, Hollandia, in May 1944.** BELOW: **Sherman tanks of the US Marine Corps moving along the shoreline after landing.**

Army could never react with sufficient speed. There were 250,000 Japanese troops in positions along the coast. MacArthur successfully bypassed over half of them, leaving pockets which, cut off from resupply or any hope of rescue, were effectively neutralized.

Some 241km/150 miles along the coast from Lae, and within range of land-based air support, Madang was expected by the enemy to be MacArthur's next objective. His sights were, however, set on Hollandia, a major administrative and logistics hub a full 805km/500 miles distant.

ABOVE: **Bulldozers were vital on soft sand, but specialist US Marine Corps beach parties kept things moving.** BELOW: **Matilda tanks of the Australian Army passing through jungle in New Guinea on a training exercise.**

The land route to Hollandia was blocked by Japanese Army concentrations at Madang and Wewak, 161km/ 100 miles further east. Operation "Reckless" would bypass both, to simultaneously hit Hollandia (manned mainly by rear-echelon troops) and Tanahmerah Bay, around 32km/20 miles to the west. The two forces would advance toward each other to take a group of three, strategically important airfields, thus releasing aircraft carriers allocated by Nimitz to provide initial air cover. A third landing would be mounted at Aitape, 161km/100 miles east of Hollandia, to seize a secondary airstrip.

The landings were made on April 22, 1944 and, despite the difficulties of landing supplies over reef-fringed shores, then on to the boggy hinterland with almost impassable tracks, all major objectives were achieved within five days. As anticipated, the defenders offered little resistance, but a potentially dangerous Japanese counter-attack from Wakde, to the west, was neatly stopped by the rapid response of a further amphibious landing by US forces in Wakde.

Further rapid moves to Biak (May 27) and the western limits of New Guinea at Noemfoor (July 2) and Sansapor (July 3) took MacArthur's forces 805km/500 miles beyond Hollandia. Organised Japanese resistance on New Guinea had ended by late August 1944. MacArthur now looked to head north for the Philippines, some 1,127km/700 miles distant, a cause for considerable disquiet in Japan, where the Tojo administration had already stepped down following the taking of Saipan in June 1944.

The most versatile craft of "MacArthur's Navy" proved to be the LSTs, which moved almost everything but the tanks for which they were designed. Smaller LCTs penetrated where LSTs could not go, their crews living aboard for long periods in improvised accommodation. Follow-up LCIs were available in reasonable numbers but most "big ships" – APA, AKA, LPD – had to be allocated as the operation demanded.

Leyte Gulf

When, on October 20, 1944, Lieutenant General Krueger's Sixth Army rolled ashore on Leyte, almost without opposition, General MacArthur had finally realized his driving ambition of returning to the Philippines. Encouraged by a perceived lack of Japanese aerial resistance, he had struck at a point halfway along the extensive Philippines archipelago. Their immediate seaward flank covered by Vice-Admiral Kinkaid's Seventh Fleet, Vice-Admiral Wilkinson and Rear-Admiral Barbey landed the US Army's II Corps on adjacent beaches at Leyte Gulf in an operation the near-perfection of which was born of hard-learned experience. Close air support was provided by Rear-Admiral Thomas Sprague's force of escort aircraft carriers (CVE) but deep cover, to prevent incursion by the Imperial Japanese Navy, was the responsibility of the powerful fleet carrier groups detached from Admiral Nimitz's 3rd Fleet. Admiral Halsey, the commander, answered to Nimitz; Kinkaid, on the other hand, was responsible to MacArthur. Although considerably reduced by nearly three years of operations, the Imperial Japanese Navy had not lost its appetite for a

"Trafalgar-like" battle that would decide, at a stroke, mastery of the Pacific. The Leyte landing triggered a pre-prepared naval battle plan of typical Japanese complexity.

The Japanese fleet would be divided into three main groups. A first group of carriers (virtually useless because of a lack of trained aircrew) would patrol north-east of the Philippines, providing a lure that the impulsive Halsey would be unable to resist. With the latter's force lured to the north, the way would be open for the other two groups to hit the 7th Fleet's amphibious force, laying at anchor in Leyte Gulf, from two directions simultaneously.

A major weakness of the Japanese plan was the reliance on land-based air support, now largely non-existent. Its creators, however, could not have forecast the divided command chains of Halsey and Kinkaid, who could communicate only with difficulty. They also could not have known that Nimitz had made

BELOW: **Japanese opposition near Dulag was sporadic but, taking no chances, this newly landed platoon was keeping under cover.**

LEFT: **The consummate showman and inspirational leader, General Douglas MacArthur, having made his carefully staged "I have returned" landing, was quick to return ashore to mingle with combat troops.**

a rare error in approving the wording of Halsey's functional directive. Certainly, the latter was ordered to destroy any enemy forces threatening the "Philippines Area", but this instruction carried a rider. "In case opportunity for destruction of major portions of the enemy fleet offers or can be created, such destruction becomes the primary task".

Halsey's carrier groups were already striking at Japanese ships approaching Leyte Gulf, but reports by his pilots of damage inflicted were over-optimistic to the point where Halsay believed that the enemy forces had been reduced to a level easily handled by Kinkaid's 7th Fleet. When a reconnaissance aircraft finally detected the decoy force, Halsey reacted exactly as the Japanese planners had anticipated and intended. Complying with Nimitz's directive, he headed northward with all four carrier groups and their battleship supporting force. Deeply involved with affairs at Leyte, Kinkaid rested comfortably in the belief that

the approaches to the gulf were controlled by the enormous power of the 3rd Fleet. Halsey omitted to appraise him of the fact his fleet was now heading away from Leyte at 30 knots.

Although the Japanese Navy's southern attack was eliminated in the night action of the Surigao Strait, the more powerful northern force left the unguarded San Bernadino Strait and headed southward toward the vulnerable (and still unaware) amphibious fleet in Leyte Gulf. By the greatest of good fortune, Sprague's escort carrier force lay in its path. A desperate and confused action ensued off Samar with US destroyers and escort carriers pitted against Japanese battleships and cruisers.

The Japanese commander, Admiral Kurita, had already been greatly uneasy at the lack of opposition to his progress and now, despite his overwhelming firepower, appeared unnerved by the ferocity of Sprague's defence. Thinking that he had actually encountered Halsey's carriers, Kurita withdrew his ships.

ABOVE: **USS *Princeton* (CVL-23) on fire, with USS *Birmingham* (CL-46) approaching to assist with firefighting.** RIGHT: **USS *Birmingham* went alongside when the bomb stowage on USS *Princeton* exploded and the vessel sank. The action took place during the Battle of Leyte Gulf, October 24, 1944.**

Operation "Detachment", Iwo Jima

The Bonin Islands offered the most direct route to the Japanese home islands. Halfway between Saipan and Tokyo, Iwo Jima was the most attractive objective, having two completed airfields and a third under construction just 1,046km/650 miles from the Japanese capital. For the Japanese, its loss would be psychologically bad as it would be the first breach in their so-called "Inner Defence Zone". Recognizing now that a final campaign on the home islands was inevitable, the Japanese high command sought time to prepare. Strategically, Iwo Jima looked a certainty as the US military's next objective. Lieutenant General Kuribayashi was sent there at the time of the Saipan invasion (June 15, 1944) with orders to turn the island into an impregnable fortress.

Less than 8 x 5km/5 x 3 miles, the island lies on a north-east, south-west axis. At the southern extremity the dormant mass of the volcano Mount Suribachi dominates a triangular-shaped zone of flat, featureless sand that offers over 3.2km/2 miles of clear beaches on either coast. The northern half of Iwo Jima is almost flat, bordered by cliff-bound shores. Iwo Jima is made up of soft volcanic rock, not coral, and easily quarried. Kuribayashi had fully exploited this facility, creating numerous artillery positions, interconnected by tunnels with deep shelters for stores and ammunition magazines.

As of February 1945, the defenders numbered some 21,000, including many naval personnel and construction units. Their orders were to resist to the end, an attritional contest for which the prize would be time gained.

ABOVE: **The characteristic shape of Iwo Jima, with Mount Suribachi at the near end. Both Japanese airfields are visible. Beaches on either shore were assaulted.**
RIGHT: **Twelve rocket-firing LSMs advanced on the beach in line abreast, each releasing 120 projectiles aimed at positions just beyond the shoreline.**

The US military did not disguise their intentions. Every day for the two months preceding the d-day of February 19, 1945, the island was bombed. For the final three days the island received heavy naval bombardment. The Japanese simply retired to their deep bunkers and waited. Offshore, Vice-Admiral Richmond K. Turner controlled no less than 495 assorted vessels and, from his headquarters ship, USS *Eldorado* (AGC-11), he watched as some 500 LVTs manoeuvred into ten assault waves. Under a rolling naval barrage and preceded by 12 rocket-armed LCS (L) the first wave hit the beach unopposed and on schedule. Within 45 minutes, some 9,000 troops were ashore, closely followed by LSMs carrying medium tanks.

ABOVE: **Guided and protected by flanking destroyers, LVTs move in toward the dust and smoke-shrouded shore. The steep beach of volcanic ash and cinders proved difficult, offering little traction for vehicles.** LEFT: **The leading wave approaching the south-eastern beach. All were covered by fire from Mount Suribachi.**

ABOVE: **Trailing blazing fuel, a Nakajima Type 97 "Kate" disintegrating under close-range fire.** RIGHT: **The wooden deck on a US Navy carrier was vulnerable to kamikaze attack, unlike the armoured deck on a British carrier.**

The model operation now, however, hit problems. The beach was backed by a soft cinder terrace, up to 4m/13ft in height and with a 45-degree slope. Vehicles could not gain traction, walking was difficult, running impossible. A rising surf swung assault craft, stranding them broadside on to the beach. Into this the Japanese directed a heavy mortar bombardment which, unlike artillery shells exploding deep in the soft sand, caused the majority of the first day's 2,400 casualties. Growing stacks of stores added to the blazing equipment along the shoreline. By nightfall, leading elements of the USMC had advanced only 500 yards inland.

By now, 30,000 men were ashore but the expected Japanese counter-attack did not materialize. Kuribayashi was conserving his strength for a hard-fought defence. Mount Suribachi, the source of much of the defensive gunfire, was taken on the fourth day, enabling the main effort to be directed northward against two defensive lines that ran the width of the island. This advance involved the commitment of some of the floating reserve. This action was supported at every stage by naval gunfire.

BELOW: **The volcanic sand beaches on Iwo Jima gave some cover for infantrymen, but were almost impassable for vehicles.**

LEFT: **The commanding view from Mount Suribachi. The total absence of cover on the beach area gives an idea of the daunting task facing the assault force on Iwo Jima. Note that the steep beach gradient necessitated LSTs to maintain "ahead" power.**

In the amphibious assembly area, vessels suffered considerably from concealed Japanese artillery while, at sea, supporting 5th Fleet warships were being attacked by kamikaze aircraft. The carriers, providing all air support, were particularly favoured targets, USS *Bismarck Sea* (CVE-95) being sunk and the veteran USS *Saratoga* (CV-3) crippled for three months by five hits within three minutes. The final outcome on Iwo Jima was never in doubt, US forces had attacked in overwhelming strength. Nonetheless, US forces suffered some 7,000 fatalities, 900 of them naval. The Japanese lost 21,000, and some 200 were captured alive.

LEFT: **A barren cinder-covered heap overlooked by the imposing spectre of Mount Suribachi. The objective of the assault was the command of two strategic airfields. This swamped LVT (A) (4) is lying alongside a Japanese wreck and the general debris at the end of an amphibious landing.**

ABOVE: **USS *Bunker Hill* was struck by two kamikaze aircraft, which caused some 400 dead and missing.** LEFT: **Task Force 58 included 17 aircraft carriers. To counter this force, the Japanese were forced to use mass kamikaze attacks.**

Operation "Iceberg", Okinawa

Okinawa is a large Pacific island, some 97km/60 miles in length and around 23km/14 miles wide. The southern half is rolling countryside, supporting the bulk of the then 450,000 indigenous population. The northern half is ruggedly mountainous. Only 563km/350 miles from the Japanese mainland, Okinawa was required for the operation of heavy bombers and as an assembly area and springboard for the planned invasion of Japan.

Operation "Iceberg" was never intended as a surprise attack, for several large airfields were within range. The task of aircraft from Mitscher's 5th Fleet carriers was to wear down enemy strength beforehand, even before it was known that massed kamikaze (suicide) attacks were planned. Several days of minesweeping preceded the first landing, where the offshore archipelago of the Kerama Retto had been captured as a forward emergency fleet base. The final six days before the main landing, on April 1, were devoted to heavy naval bombardment.

The amphibious operation followed a, by now, near-standard procedure that varied only to take into account local topographical differences. The assault, in the south-west, was on a 10km/6 mile front and adjacent to two major airfields.

ABOVE: **A medium-calibre coast defence gun spiked by the invaders. There were many such hidden bunkers built by the Japanese on Okinawa.** LEFT: **The deep and soft volcanic sand, which made up the steep beach on Okinawa, caused serious problems for the first wave of the attacking US Marines. Vehicles could not negotiate the beach until later in the operation, after metal matting had been laid.**

ABOVE: **The island of Okinawa was in the main very rocky. The landscape was totally unlike that of the coral atolls or the volcanic island of Iwo Jima.**

Against negligible opposition, the leading LCI (G) support craft moved through the anchored bombardment ships, approaching the beach in line abreast, followed by patrol craft marshalling the lines of following LVTs.

The leading line of the turreted and armoured LVT (A) was followed at strict six-minute intervals by five lines of standard ramp-equipped, troop-carrying LVTs. All cleared any obstructing reefs and landed the main assault waves within 30 minutes. Next were LSMs carrying Sherman tanks, then LCIs with follow-up infantry.

By the end of "L-Day", over 50,000 troops were ashore, virtually without loss. Occupying the island, however, would take until June 22, by which time 7,600 US troops would have been killed, together with 4,900 seamen lost in 368 ships sunk or damaged by air attack. No less than 131,000 Japanese troops died in the ferocious fighting.

ABOVE: **The great strength of the LVT was the ability to land troops beyond the vulnerable beach zone.** BELOW: **Initial waves hit the beach on time at 08:30, finding little direct opposition. By 16:00, some 50,000 troops were ashore, and the operation had proceeded with deceptive ease.**

DUKW

Although not a vessel, the DUKW was to become a vital element in any amphibious force, and one of the most useful vehicles in World War II.

The type was the brainchild of a civilian engineer Roger W. Hofheims, whose first project had been the Aqua-Cheetah. This was an amphibious vehicle powered by a mid-mounted Ford V8 engine driving all four wheels by chains. In later versions Dodge WC axles were used. Although improved, the vehicle was not accepted by the US Army.

The concept of an amphibious truck was taken up by the National Defense Research Committee (NDRC) and a prototype ordered from General Motors Corporation (GMC)

ABOVE: **A supply depot on the Normandy beachhead a day after the landings on June 6, 1944. DUKW vehicles were also used to move troops and supplies inland. They were truly versatile amphibians, and remained in service after World War II.**

and boat designers Sparkman & Stephens. The vehicle was initially built on the AFKWX353 military truck chassis with the body designed by Roderick Stephens Jr.

In October 1942, an order was placed for 2,000 of the type to be built on the GMC CCKW353, with the amphibious version being coded as DUKW (D: 1942, U: amphibian, K: all-wheel drive, W: dual rear axles). Almost immediately it was named "Duck" by US troops.

The vehicle was first used at New Caledonia, March 1943, and again for Operation "Torch". Later in 1943, the British Eighth Army deployed 230 DUKWs for the landings

ABOVE: **First used in the Pacific at Kwajalein, New Caledonia, the DUKW, like the LVT, could negotiate offshore reefs. Here, as cargo carriers, the vehicles are coming ashore directly from transport ships. Capable of carrying 2 tons of cargo, the DUKW was described by US Admiral Turner as "the Army's most important contribution to the technique of amphibious warfare".**

ABOVE AND RIGHT: **Two DUKWs could be linked, providing the necessary buoyancy and platform to support a 10-ton vehicle. Vehicle wheels were guided in two narrow and shallow ramps.**

on Sicily. The type was used to ferry troops and supplies from transport ships to the beach. Once a beachhead had been established DUKWs were then used to move supplies inland.

Over 2,000 DUKWs were used for the Normandy landings on June 6, 1944. The vehicles were to transport 3,500,000 tons of supplies and equipment into France and Belgium between June 1944 and July 1945.

A total of 21,147 of the type were built and many were to remain in service with the armies of the USA, Canada, the UK and the USSR for many years after World War II. Further vehicles were supplied to the postwar armies of France, the Netherlands, Belgium and West Germany.

BELOW: **DUKWs shared the weakness of early assault craft for, lacking ramps, heavily equipped troops were required to leap 1.8m/6ft. Like an LCVP, a DUKW could be fitted within an LCM (3), or it could easily be carried under davits.**

LEFT: **The approach to Inchon was through poorly charted mudflats, subject to a 11m/36ft tidal range. Therefore, very large numbers of standard and armoured LVTs were used in addition to LCVPs and only eight LSTs.**

Operation "Chromite", Inchon, Korea

Freed from 35 years of Japanese domination, Korea was divided post-war into a communist North and a democratic South. The latter, with only nominal defence forces, but allied to the United States, was suddenly invaded by North Korea in overwhelming strength on June 25, 1950.

Lately Supreme Commander, South West Pacific, General Douglas MacArthur was now effectively ruling Japan as C-in-C, US Army of Occupation. With the United National Security Council's condemnation of the North Korean action, MacArthur was created C-in-C of the newly reactivated US Eighth Army. Elements were quickly mobilized to assist South Korean forces but, no longer battle-hardened, they performed poorly. Within weeks, all were confined to a small pocket around the south-eastern port of Pusan. The US military moved urgently, meanwhile, to reactivate seasoned reservists, "mothballed" ships, aircraft and armour.

Despite vociferous doubters, MacArthur insisted once again that his policy should be to attack the enemy by surprise, rather than dissipate reinforcements in holding and developing the Pusan pocket. He impressed upon US Chiefs of Staff that the North Koreans, while fanatical to their cause, had no combat experience or any knowledge of manoeuvre warfare. Ninety per cent of their strength, he said, was concentrated around the Pusan perimeter, where their prime intention was devoted to pushing the defending forces into the sea.

While the Eighth Army was still able to hold the perimeter, MacArthur intended to make an amphibious landing over 161km/100 miles distant at Inchon on the west coast. From here the South Korean capital, Seoul, could quickly be recaptured, whereupon the two forces would break out and link up. With lines of communication already extended, the North Koreans would now find themselves cut off and, MacArthur stated, would panic.

Inchon, however, was a difficult objective, situated at the head of miles of river channels that wound tortuous routes through vast mudflats subject to tidal ranges of up to 11m/36ft and 5-knot currents. Approaching LSTs required 8.8m/29ft of water, which immediately determined both the date and time. The situation was urgent.

Commanding the immediate approaches to Inchon is the island of Wolmi. Following three days of air and naval bombardment, and a final attack from three, rocket-firing LSMs,

ABOVE: **Because Inchon was in occupied "friendly" territory, the 45-minute pre-landing naval bombardment had to be very precisely targeted on the docks area.**

LEFT: **Four LSTs beached at low water. Men and equipment were being loaded on to Red Beach one day after the initial landing.**

the 500-man garrison was overcome by a somewhat improvised force of three APDs, 17 LCVPs and three tank-carrying LCUs, launched from a single LSD. Just 20 US Marines were injured.

One tide, and a necessary six hours later, the main landing was staged at Inchon. The main landing depended upon eight ageing LSTs, lately operated by Japanese crews, the only vessels that could be deployed in the time available.

As Inchon was occupied "friendly" territory, the 45-minute preliminary bombardment had to be precisely targeted on the port area in order to minimize civilian casualties. The "beaches" were bounded by stone seawalls up to 4.6m/15 feet in height, major obstructions to the US Marine-laden LVTs and LCUs launched from LSDs. One LST hit the wall so hard that it was breached, allowing troops to disembark. Further breaches in the seawalls were made by using explosive charges.

Toward evening, mist, smoke and drizzle hastened the darkness. Fortunately, resistance was light, for all LSTs had to remain aground until the following tide. With the dawn, Allied air superiority was asserted and reinforcements came ashore. Within days, the UN main forces had linked up and, its spirit broken, the North Korean Army had begun a rapid withdrawal back to the security of the north.

MacArthur's gamble, his total faith in his own judgement and in the qualities of his remaining veterans of World War II, totally changed the course of the war, although, at this stage, it was very far from being decided. Following World War II, several senior military figures had predicted that amphibious warfare was outmoded. Inchon changed all that and a service that had come to be neglected gained a new recognition.

ABOVE: **The enormous tide range is clearly illustrated in this image of stranded landing craft.** RIGHT: **A McDonnell FH2-H Banshee flying over Korea, 1952. The type served with the US Navy and the US Marine Corps first as an escort fighter for US bombers, then for ground attack and photographic reconnaissance.**

LEFT: **The first-ever helicopter-borne assault was mounted from the British light fleet carriers HMS *Theseus* and HMS *Ocean*. The half-battalion-sized force was augmented by an Anglo-French paratroop landing.** BELOW: **A pall of smoke from burning oil tanks opposite Port Fuad provided a landmark throughout the landings.**

Operation "Musketeer", Suez

For the greater part of a century, the Suez Canal had functioned largely under Anglo-French control. In July 1956, however, the Egyptian president, General Gamal Nasser, unilaterally announced its nationalization, an action that brought the British and French governments to plan military action to effect not only the canal's recovery but also probable régime change in Egypt. In order to intervene in a manner that world opinion would accept as legitimate, a devious pact was agreed with Israel, whereby the latter would first attack Egypt. Pleading the "international importance" of the waterway, a joint Anglo-French ultimatum would then demand a ceasefire, to be followed immediately by forces of these nations moving in to "safeguard" the zone immediately bordering the canal.

An amphibious assault over the beaches fronting Port Said (at the canal's northern entrance) would coincide with British and French parachute drops to seize vital airfields

and key bridges. Reinforcements and heavy equipment would follow up immediately through captured Egyptian airfields and port facilities.

The British Parachute Brigade had not conducted recent drops, nor had the Royal Marine Commando Brigade practised amphibious landing. For the one there were insufficient transport aircraft, and the other a shortage of landing craft. Much of the equipment was from reserves "mothballed" at the end of World War II.

Recommissioning, assembly and specialized training took time (the French had to recall their only LSD from the Far East). This meant that the operation, following several revisions, could not be undertaken before November, 1956. The whole undertaking was politically driven. The physical scale and protracted time frame made both governments'

LEFT: **Blockships scuttled by the Egyptians to block the entrance to the Suez Canal at Port Said, photographed from a Royal Navy aircraft.**

ABOVE: **Not yet a well-practised exercise, troop and equipment movements on the flight deck on HMS *Ocean* appeared disorganized.** BELOW: **French troops in LVT (4), patrolling the deserted town of Port Fuad. All Allied vehicles were painted with a white "H" identifying letter.**

ABOVE: **Westland S-55 Whirlwind helicopters on the deck of HMS *Theseus*. A French Navy hospital ship can be seen in the background.**

intentions abundantly clear and world opinion became increasingly hostile, a situation skilfully exploited by government-controlled Radio Cairo.

The landing beaches had a very shallow slope so LSTs would need port facilities to discharge. The first wave, which went ashore at 04:50 on November 6 were embarked in 16 LVTs, dating from World War II, all that was available. Fortunately, opposition was limited for the second wave of LCAs (many of them ancient LCA [1]), grounded some distance out. This left the commandos to wade ashore before crossing a wide, open beach. The four LCTs that followed had to offload Centurion tanks into 1.5m/5ft of water. Quickly captured, however, the adjacent harbour basin permitted follow-up LCTs and LSTs to discharge at the quayside. Owing to the proximity of the civil population, only carefully controlled and very limited gunfire support from destroyers could be employed.

The US Marine Corps had been investigating the use of helicopters for the rapid insertion of spearhead forces, the technique being termed "Vertical Envelopment". Two British light fleet carriers thus joined the invasion fleet with a helicopter force embarked and with the intention of putting theory into practice. To the force commanders, however, the lift capacity did not match the anticipated opposition. The assault tasks were

allocated, successfully, to paratroops. A half-battalion-sized commando was, nonetheless, flown ashore within 90 minutes, with the carriers a distant 16km/10 miles offshore.

Although some Egyptian positions resisted, Allied forces were well supported by carrier aircraft. These along with aircraft operating from Cyprus, destroyed most of the Egyptians' Soviet-built aircraft in pre-emptive strikes against airfields.

Major crossings secured, armoured forces quickly headed out of Port Said and down the canal, already littered with blockships. International public opinion, led by the USA, had almost immediately called upon the British and French governments to desist. The British War Cabinet's resolve to continue was quickly broken, the French having to follow suit.

Committed to war by their politicians, and now disgusted to be let down by them, British and French forces ceased fire at 12:00 on November 7, barely 30 hours after the first landing. Operation "Musketeer" had been militarily successful, resulting in something of a renewal of Britain's run-down amphibious warfare capabilities.

ABOVE: **Peace observers from the United Nations Organization (UNO) arriving in Port Said on November 14, 1956, to supervise the front at El Cap.**

LEFT: **USS *Cabildo* (LSD-16) carried 5,500 troops of the 9th Marine Amphibious Brigade to An Thuang.**

Operation "Starlite", Vietnam

Much of the amphibious warfare in Vietnam was carried out in its many muddy creeks. From time to time operations inland were integrated with over-the-beach landings staged by the Amphibious Ready Group (ARG) of the 7th Fleet, which transported units of the Marine Special Landing Force (SLF).

Although US Marine Corps (USMC) advisors had served with Vietnamese regular forces since 1955, it was only in March 1965 that USMC units were established ashore to counter growing Viet Cong (VC) influence.

The operation was launched on August 17, 1965 by 5,500 troops of the 9th Marine Amphibious Brigade (MAB) made up of the 2nd Battalion, 4th Marines; 3rd Battalion, 4th Marines; 3rd Battalion, 3rd Marines; and 3rd Battalion, 7th Marines.

Not yet fully appreciating that its strength lay in guerrilla warfare, the VC had formed the 1st Regiment, which, estimated at some 1,500, was located near Chu Lai. Intelligence indicated that its objective was 3rd MAB although, considering US military superiority in mobility and firepower, this was a risky strategy .

With Operation "Starlite", US forces suddenly took the initiative, exploiting the enemy's tendency to view a coastal peninsula as a position of strength. In this case, the enemy was based in an area of some 10 x 5km/6 x 3 miles. If the VC felt that the seaward flank was unassailable, however,

ABOVE: **USS *Galveston* (CL-93/CLG-3) was positioned offshore to provide any required supporting gunfire.**
RIGHT: **A Sampan of the US Navy's 15 Junk Division, which operated in South Vietnam waters, alongside a locally crewed Sampan. These vessels were intercepted to stop the supply of ammunition or other supplies to Viet Cong forces.**

LEFT: **The LVTE-1 version of the "Amtrac" was used for the first time on Operation "Starlite". The toothed-plough on the front of the vehicle was used to dig up mines and other explosives buried in the beach.**

they had overlooked the 7th Fleet which, on August 18, put a Battalion Landing Team (BLT) at regiment strength over the beach on the left flank of the VC positions.

A second BLT was landed by helicopter over three landing zones (LZ) to block the routes inland, while a third group used LVTs to cross the river that marked the right flank of VC positions. The light artillery fire from elements of 3rd Battalion, 12th Marines was augmented by naval support fire, available at any point along the coast, while carrier-based USMC air support flew unchallenged above. The VC forces were trapped and, over the next six days, would lose nearly 1,000 fighters, a fatality "exchange rate" of over 25:1.

In a bloody lesson, the Viet Cong learned to contain over-confidence and to avoid the sort of pitched battle that greatly favoured the US military tactics.

BELOW: **Aircraft of the US Navy and US Marine Corps were used to attack the beach prior to the landing, and later for air support.**

ABOVE: **Troops of the 9th Marine Amphibious Division landing on An Thuong beach from an LVT vehicle.** BELOW: **Viet Cong prisoners awaiting transport by USMC helicopter to the rear area for interrogation.**

Operation "Corporate", Falklands

The Falklands was very much a tale of two landings: one amphibious operation secured the islands, another regained them. Beset by civil unrest, the military junta in control of the Argentine Government decided to refocus hostile opinion on to a universally popular cause, that of occupying the distant Falkland Islands, claimed (as the Malvinas) since 1833.

Some 402km/250 miles from mainland Argentina, the Falklands are nearly 322km/200 miles across. The group is formed from many islands, all rugged and with deep sea inlets. Most of their area is concentrated in the East and West Falklands, separated by the wide Falkland Sound. Population is sparse, settlements and roads almost non-existent. Incorporating Government House and the islands' main airfield, the capital, Port Stanley, is at the eastern extremity of East Falkland.

British military presence usually stood at the strength of one Royal Marine platoon. In April 1982, it was being relieved, so two platoons, totalling 69 men, were available.

With their national airline providing the islands' only air link, Argentine intelligence was well served. General Galtieri, president and Army C-in-C, decided wisely to act with minimum force but in overwhelming strength. For this the 700-strong 2nd Marine Infantry Battalion sufficed, embarked with their 19 US-supplied LVTs in the only available LST and two transports.

Port Stanley is located on the central inlet of three parallel sea inlets, and can be approached from any direction. During the night of April 1/2, 1982, a destroyer landed 50 Argentine Special Forces personnel some 3.2km/2 miles south of Port Stanley. These split, one group attacking the empty Royal Marine barracks to the west of the town, the other simultaneously surrounding Government House. Following a covert reconnaissance conducted by a submarine party, the main landing was made to the north of Port Stanley. Troops in the LVTs stopped only to secure the airfield before moving on to approach Port Stanley from the east.

ABOVE: **RAF Chinook helicopters were too heavy for the decks of the LPD, and usually remained at the hover when loading supplies to be moved ashore.**

ABOVE: **Following the well-proven US Marine Corps dictum of surprise, British forces landed at San Carlos Water without opposition.** LEFT: **To move the troops of the invasion force, the British government requisitioned a number of civilian ships. SS** *Canberra*, **a P&O liner, was used to transport No. 4 Commando, 3 Commando Brigade, Royal Marines to the Falkland Islands.**

LEFT: **HMS *Plymouth*, a Type 12 frigate, on fire and badly damaged after being hit by four bombs during an air attack by Argentine aircraft. A Type 21 frigate, HMS *Avenger*, is close by, and Royal Marines are moving in an LCM (9) to provide rescue for the crew of the damaged ship.**

Following reports of darkened vessels offshore, the Royal Marines had already concentrated around Government House and the town's eastern approaches. At each location a brisk exchange of fire saw the invaders take casualties. The Argentines, however, adhered closely to their "minimum force" orders, and warships available for gunfire support were not required. At 09:25, with the situation hopeless, Governor Rex Hunt ordered a ceasefire. Following the well-planned operation the Argentine flag was at last raised over the renamed *Islas Malvinas*. Transports were already off-loading heavy equipment

ABOVE: **Flying the traditional "Jolly Roger" flag to indicate a victory, HMSub *Conqueror* returning to Faslane, Scotland on July 3, 1982. The nuclear-powered vessel was used to sink the Argentine Navy cruiser *General Belgrano* (ex-USS *Phoenix* [CL-46]) on May 2, 1982.**

and, within two hours, Lockheed C-130 Hercules transports began to touch down with the first elements of the 25th Infantry Regiment, to become the garrison force.

For months previously, Argentina's increasingly bellicose behaviour in the region had provided numerous "clear warnings", but the British government appears not to have warned President Galtieri informally that any permanent territorial ambitions would be met with summary eviction. The British lack of firm action must be blamed, therefore, for Argentina's escalating boldness.

The government of Margaret Thatcher was riven by disloyalty and division. Whether, like Galtieri, the prime minister relied on the unifying potential of a decision to go to war, or whether she was simply being stubborn, remains a point of debate. Encouraged by support from the UN Security Council and assurances from the First Sea Lord that the Royal Navy could handle the situation, she made the commitment to remove Argentinian forces from the Falklands.

In truth, the Royal Navy had already been considerably weakened by many Defence Reviews, and was due to suffer further. Future cuts were to include the two LPDs, some if not all of the six LSLs and the recently completed carriers. The design of this type had resulted from the obvious shortcomings found at Suez in 1956.

For "measured response" there was no time and the "Task Force" that sailed southward on the longest-range amphibious operation in history (12,874km/8,000 miles) was largely a sequence of ships leaving as available. All were supported by the Royal Fleet Auxiliary (RFA) and a diverse range of Ships Taken Up From Trade (STUFT). The requirement for speed meant they were not combat loaded and the South Atlantic island of Ascension became the base for regrouping and loading.

The British were in two-brigade strength. The 3 Commando Brigade, amphibious-trained, left with the first part of the task force. It was followed by the 5th Infantry Brigade, which had not been trained in amphibious warfare.

The location for an amphibious assault, as fully expected by the Argentines, was to the south-west of Stanley. The actual choice was the unlikely San Carlos Water, 80km/50 miles distant and opening on to Falkland Sound. Beyond surprise, the location had the advantages of being undefended yet easily defensible. The excellent anchorage was surrounded by hills that made the enemy's use of missiles impossible. Inserted special forces had reported no evidence of the area being mined, and the route to Port Stanley was accessible by sea.

Argentina could deploy more, and superior aircraft, but, operating so far from their mainland bases, these could not loiter over the target. This allowed the two British aircraft carriers to establish a tentative local air superiority zone. Transport helicopters, crucial to manoeuvre warfare, were in desperately short supply following the sinking of the MV *Atlantic Conveyor* by two air-launched Exocet missiles.

A critical task for the Royal Navy was to prevent the Argentine fleet from intervening. This was achieved by the ruthless, but logical, sinking of the cruiser ARA *General Belgrano* by HMSub *Conqueror*. Thereafter, fear of nuclear-powered attack submarines kept the enemy's surface ships out of range.

The Argentines did not exploit the vulnerability of long British Sealines of Communication (SLOC) to submarine attack, but their fighter-bombers were a major threat, with

ABOVE: **Although having to follow a predictable flight path, pilots of McDonnell Douglas A4 Skyhawk aircraft of the Argentine Navy were able to stage fast and low bombing runs on British ships.**
LEFT: **In deceptively placid surroundings, close-in under high ground, a large commercial vessel is being unloaded by Westland Sea King helicopters.**

LEFT: **Troops unloading mortar ammunition from a Westland Wessex helicopter of the Royal Navy in preparation for the battle to retake enemy positions.**

frequent and skilful low-level attacks. Airborne Early Warning (AEW) aircraft of the Fleet Air Arm had been scrapped as a government cost-cutting measure. Advance warning of strikes utilized US-supplied intelligence, naval surveillance destroyers and special forces teams located in forward positions.

The combination of Harrier aircraft and Sidewinder air-to-air missiles (AAM) proved lethal to the raiding aircraft but, due to a shortage of war stocks, extra supplies of the missiles needed to be urgently procured from the USA.

On May 21, 3 Commando Brigade landed unopposed at San Carlos Water but had to await the arrival and reorganization of the 5th Brigade. With the British public learning daily of ships lost and damaged, London demanded rapid military success, leading directly to a decisive battle at Goose Green.

The direct thrust by 3 Commando Brigade across East Falkland was complemented by activity of 5th Infantry Brigade along the coastal route. To put the enemy off

balance, part of the latter was shipped up the coast, to Fitzroy in the two LSLs. The enemy had Bluff Cove under observation and air attack soon followed. Apparently unfamiliar with the lessons of history, senior officers had refused to order a rapid disembarkation as first priority. The ensuing air strike was devastating, resulting in the single greatest loss of life to the British in the Falklands campaign.

Under open skies 3 Commando Brigade was also vulnerable to air attack but the Argentines made poor use of the Pucara, an excellent ground-attack aircraft.

Naval gunfire support was widely used, not only in direct support but also to confuse, harass and distract the enemy. Several pinpoint actions were necessary to dislodge the Argentine forces from various hills overlooking Port Stanley and its approaches. This achieved, the outcome of the final battle was never in doubt. On June 14, the British forces took the surrender of over 10,000 Argentine troops.

ABOVE: **HMS *Invincible* off the Falkland Islands, June 12, 1982. On deck are Sea Harrier FRS-1 aircraft of No. 801 and No. 809 Squadron, Fleet Air Arm.**

ABOVE: **HMS *Hermes*, the flagship of the Falklands Fleet. On deck are Harrier GR3s of No. 1 Squadron, Royal Air Force and Sea Harriers of No. 800 Squadron, Fleet Air Arm.**

The Middle East and current trends

Amphibious warfare came of age with the great operations of World War II which, by 1945, had defined the method to such an extent that doctrine changed little throughout the ensuing Cold War era. While this confrontation contained a real threat, this was outweighed in the West by the realities of restricted defence budgets. The British configured the Royal Navy primarily around a North Atlantic anti-submarine force. Starved of funds, the numbers of amphibious elements gradually shrank. Only the US military maintained an efficient amphibious force. Even the USA, as was evident in the 1950 landing at Inchon, Korea, had to draw on reserves to meet an emergency.

At Suez in 1956, the British used the small number of World War II surplus vessels that remained serviceable. Thanks to considerable ingenuity, and a lack of real opposition, the operation was successful, only to be let down by political pressures. Suez taught the sharp lesson that the world order had changed and that independent action was no longer possible without the approval of the United Nations and/or the USA.

Britain's commitment was to be tested in 1961 when Kuwait, in which Britain had enormous investment, was threatened with immediate invasion by the military dictatorship in neighbouring Iraq. Despite an agreement to underwrite Kuwait's defence, Britain could not move in a deterrent force for fear of appearing "aggressive". This was precisely what was required, as Iraq could mount an occupation of Kuwait in a matter of hours.

Warlike threats, however, had continued for so long that the British were able to make preparatory moves, although even the capacity to deploy a reinforced brigade group involved almost world-wide repositioning. When the Emir of Kuwait was finally persuaded to request assistance it was thus assembled quickly. Lack of suitable vessels saw troops needing to be flown in. Transport Command (RAF), immediately overstretched, had to charter commercial aircraft. It was also quickly discovered that otherwise friendly states, fearful of appearing partial, would vacillate over the question of rights to over-fly their territory.

ABOVE: **USS San Antonio (LPD-17) with USS Carter Hall (LSD-50) and guided missile destroyer USS Roosevelt (DDG-80) transiting the Atlantic Ocean on September 6, 2008.** LEFT: **A McDonnell Douglas AV-8B of the US Marine Corps approaching to land on USS Essex (LHD-2) during an exercise at Sasebo, Japan, on February 5, 2007.**

ABOVE: **Oil-funded states have no need for sophisticated weapons industries; military equipment and technology is purchased to meet a perceived level of threat.** LEFT: **An LVTP (7) launching from the docking well of a US Navy LPD.**

In 1990, Iraqi forces did overrun Kuwait, further threatening Saudi Arabia. This aggression triggered an immediate UN Security Council Resolution, allowing the USA to move significant strength into Saudi Arabia.

While leading command elements were flown in, using the by-now available Lockheed C-5 Galaxy and Lockheed C-141 Starlifter transport aircraft, the US Navy was able to quickly deploy the new Amphibious Ready Groups (ARG). Covered by a carrier strike group, an ARG was centred on a 30,000-ton helicopter assault ship (LHA) supported by an LSD, an LPD and two LSTs. Each ARG is capable of lifting a battalion-size Marine Expeditionary Unit (MEU). The rapid compilation of a full, multi-battalion Marine Expeditionary Force (MEF) was facilitated by the availability of fully loaded, pre-positioned ships, from bases in the Indian Ocean.

Such massive coalition military forces had been concentrated ashore, that the counter-attack became, essentially, a land campaign. The amphibious forces remained offshore as a floating reserve, but staged flanking strikes against the Iraqi forces. Such a continuous threat tied down considerable numbers of enemy troops. One reason for keeping these ships offshore was the heavy damage caused by mines to two valuable ships, an LPH and a CG. These incidents were a sobering reminder of how even such basic weaponry can threaten the most complex of sophisticated, multi-function ships.

ABOVE: **HMS *Albion* with HMS *Ocean* on manoeuvres. The long-range options for the type will be severely limited if the planned Royal Navy fleet carriers are cancelled as a result of threatened economic measures.**

With the collapse of the USSR and the end of the Cold War, fleets of the navies in the West had to reassess their amphibious capability and even fight government to maintain a force. The somewhat vague concept of the "international war on terror" filled the vacuum with navies moving from hi-tech ocean warfare to intervention strategy, with emphasis on home-waters warfare, while maintaining the ability to move complete military units at short notice. Joint expeditionary and carrier strike groups, carrying battalion, even brigade-sized forces, have thus replaced the earlier battle groups. This may yet change, with China and India seeking to be identified as regional military powers.

LEFT: **Major fleets have invested heavily in specialist amphibious vessels for intervention-type warfare. Two LCACs of the US Navy are shown here operating from a Wasp-class amphibious assault ship.**

91

Glossary

AGC Amphibious Command Ship (US); LCC from 1969.

AKA Attack Cargo Ship (US); LKA from 1969.

ALC Earlier designation of LCA.

"Amtrac" Popular term for LVT.

APA Attack Transport (US); LPA from 1969.

APD Auxiliary Personnel Destroyer (US); later High-Speed Transport Destroyer.

ARG Amphibious Ready Group (US).

ATG Amphibious Task Group.

AUV Autonomous Underwater Vehicle.

ballast Additional weight taken aboard to improve stability, to correct trim or to modify ship movement.

bandstand Raised island platform for gun mounting.

beam Width of hull at waterline at Standard Displacement.

bhp Brake horsepower. Power available at output of a diesel engine.

bunkers In the modern sense, fuel, rather than the compartments in which it is stored.

BYMS British Yard Minesweeper. Variant on YMS (US).

C3 (C-3) US Marine Commission designation for a cargo ship of between 137–152m/450–500ft waterline length and carrying less than 100 passengers. Note also

the "C" referred to standard cargo vessels of under 122m/400ft, C2 of 122–137m/400–450ft, and C4 of 152–168m/500–550ft.

camber Transverse curvature of a ship's deck.

cantilever Overhung structure supported at only one side or end.

casing (funnel) Outer plating surrounding exhaust end of uptakes.

CATF Commander, Amphibious Task Force (Naval).

chine Line of intersection between sides and bottom of a flat-bottomed or planing craft.

C-in-C Commander-in-Chief.

CIWS Close-In Weapon System. Close-range, anti-missile defence of automatic guns and/or missiles on single mounting.

CLF Commander, Landing Force (Marine).

CTOL Conventional Take-Off and Land.

Daihatsu Common name for a range of Japanese landing craft.

DASH Drone Anti-Submarine Helicopter.

DD tank Duplex-Drive amphibious tank.

deadweight (tonnage) Actual carrying capacity of a cargo ship, expressed usually in tons of 2,240lb. Abbreviated to "dwt".

derrick Pivoted spar, fitted with winches, for lifting loads. In US, a "cargo boom".

displacement, full load or "deep" Weight of ship (in tons of 2,240lb) when fully equipped, stored and fuelled.

displacement, standard Weight of ship less fuel and other deductions allowed by treaty.

draught (or draft) Mean depth of water in which a ship may float freely.

DUKW Amphibious truck, commonly known as a "Duck".

ECM Electronic Countermeasures.

ELINT Electronic Intelligence.

endurance Usually equal to twice the operational radius.

EOD Explosive Ordnance Disposal.

ESM Electronic Support Measures.

flare Outward curvature of hull plating.

freeboard Correctly, the vertical height between the waterline and the lowest watertight deck. Commonly, the vertical height of the shell plating from the waterline at any particular point.

gross registered tons Measure of volumetric capacity of a merchant ship. One gross ton equals 100cu ft (2.83m³) of reckonable space. Abbreviated to "grt".

"Hedgerow" "Hedgehog"-type anti-submarine spigot mortar adapted for beach mine clearance.

HMT Her Majesty's Transport.

horsepower (hp) Unit of power equal to 746 watts.

ihp Indicated horsepower. Specifically, the power delivered by the pistons of a reciprocating steam engine.

IMS Inshore Minesweeper.

knuckle Line of change in direction of shell plating. Usually a signature-reduction measure, but also reduces excessive width of upper deck in hulls of pronounced flare.

LAMPS Light Airborne Multi-Purpose System.

LASH Lighter Aboard Ship.

LCA Landing Craft, Assault.

LCA (HR) Landing Craft, Assault (Hedgerow).

LCAC Landing Craft, Air Cushion.

LCC Landing Craft, Control (UK); AGC after 1969 (US).

ABOVE: **The Royal Navy aircraft carrier HMS** *Ark Royal* **conducting a Replenishment at Sea (RAS) with the Royal Fleet Auxiliary supply vessel RFA** *Wave Knight* **in the North Sea. HMS** *Ark Royal* **was withdrawn from Royal Navy service in October 2010.**

LCF Landing Craft, FlaK.

LCG (L)/(M) Landing Craft, Gun (Large)/(Medium).

LCH Landing Craft, Headquarters (UK); British equivalent of AGC/LCC (US).

LCI (L)/(S) Landing Craft, Infantry (Large)/(Small).

LCI (R) Landing Craft, Infantry (Rocket).

LCM Landing Craft, Mechanized.

LCN Landing Craft, Navigation (UK).

LCP (L)/(M)/(S) Landing Craft, Personnel (Large)/(Medium)/(Small).

LCP (R) Landing Craft, Personnel (Ramped).

LCS (L)/(M)/(S) Landing Craft, Support (Large)/(Medium)/(Small).

LCS (R) Landing Craft, Support (Rocket) (UK).

LCT Landing Craft, Tank.

LCU Landing Craft, Utility.

LCV Landing Craft, Vehicle.

LCVP Landing Craft, Vehicle, Personnel.

length (bp) Length between perpendiculars. Customarily the distance between forward extremity of waterline at standard displacement and forward side of rudder post. For US warships, lengths on designed waterline and between perpendiculars are synonymous.

length (oa) Length, overall.

length (wl) Length, waterline. Measured at standard displacement

LSC Landing Ship, Carrier (Derrick Hoistings) (UK).

LSD Landing Ship, Dock.

LSDV Swimmer Delivery Vehicle.

LSF Landing Ship, Fighter Direction.

LSG Landing Ship, Gantry (UK).

LSH Landing Ship, Headquarters (UK).

LSI (L)/(M)/(S) Landing Ship, Infantry (Large)/(Medium)/(Small) (UK).

LSM Landing Ship, Medium.

LSM (R) Landing Ship, Medium (Rocket).

LSS Landing Ship, Sternchute (UK).

LST Landing Ship, Tank.

LVT Landing Vehicle, Tracked.

MAB Marine Amphibious Brigade (US).

MAF Marine Amphibious Force (US).

MAU Marine Amphibious Unit (US).

MCMV Mine Countermeasures Vessel (UK).

"Mexeflote" Powered pontoon used also as causeway unit (UK).

MGB Motor Gun Boat (UK).

ABOVE: **A Landing Craft, Air Cushion (LCAC) from USS *Bonhomme Richard* (LHD-6) of Expeditionary Strike Group Five (ESG-5) supporting Operation Unified Assistance, the humanitarian operation effort in the wake of the tsunami on Sumatra, Indonesia, January 10, 2005.**

ML Motor Launch (UK).

MLC Early designation of LCM.

MMS Motor Minesweeper (UK).

Monitor Shallow-draught vessel with heavy armament.

MSC Military Sealift Command (US).

MSB Minesweeping Boat (US).

MTB Motor Torpedo Boat (UK); US equivalent PT.

NATO North Atlantic Treaty Organization.

NGS Naval Gunfire Support.

OTH Over The Horizon.

PCF *see* Swift Boat.

PDMS Point Defence Missile System. Rapid-response, close-range anti-air missile system.

Plan Orange US plan for war against Japan.

protection In this context, usually only splinter-proof, but variable.

RAF Royal Air Force.

RCT Royal Corps of Transport.

RFA Royal Fleet Auxiliary.

ROV Remotely Operated Vehicle. Usually with umbilical.

SAM Surface-to-Air Missile.

sheer Curvature of deckline in fore-and-aft direction, usually upward toward either end.

shp Shaft horsepower. Power at point in shaft ahead of stern gland. Does not include frictional losses in stern gland and A-bracket.

sided Situated at sides of ship, usually as opposed to centerline location.

SIGINT Signal Intelligence.

ski jump Pronounced upward curvature at forward end of flightdeck, to enhance effect of short take-off run.

SSM Surface-to-Surface Missile.

stability range Total range through which, from a position of equilibrium, a vessel is stable in the static condition.

STUFT Ships Taken Up From Trade.

SWATH Small Waterplane Area, Twin Hull.

Swift Boat Otherwise PCF; 50ft coastal surveillance boat (Vietnam).

TF Task Force.

TG Task Group.

trim Amount by which a vessel deviates, in the fore-and-aft axis, from the designed draught.

TU Task Unit.

turbo-electric Propulsion system in which a steam turbine drives an electrical generator. This supplies energy via a cable to a propulsion motor coupled to the propeller shaft.

UAV Unmanned Aerial Vehicle.

uptake Conduit exhausting products of combustion to the funnel.

volume critical Vessel whose design is driven by space rather than weight considerations.

V/STOL Vertical or Short Take-Off and Land.

Warsaw Pact Eastern military bloc, essentially a counter to NATO.

weight critical Vessel whose design is driven by weight rather than space considerations.

Index

A
AAV, Marine Corps 9
Airborne Early Warning (AEW)
    aircraft 88
airborne landings 35, 43, 82
aircraft
    F2H-2 Banshee 32, 81
    F4U-5 Corsair 29
    FJ-4 Fury 32
    Hawker-Siddeley Sea
        Harrier 89
    kamikaze attacks 35, 74,
        75, 76
    Lockheed C-5 Galaxy 91
    Lockheed Hercules 87
    Lockheed C-141
        Starlifter 91
    McDonnell Douglas
        AV-8B 90
    McDonnell Douglas A4
        Skyhawk 88
    Nakajima Type 97 Kate 74
    Supermarine Seafire 46
    see also helicopters
Albion 91
Aleutian Islands 49
Alexander, General Harold 45
Almaack 66
Amethyste 33
amphibious forces 32–3
amphibious operations
        categories 8
        command and control
            30–1
        planning 28–9
Amphibious Ready Group
        (ARG) 84, 91
Amphibious Task Forces (ATF)
        30, 32–3
Amphibious Task Groups
        (ATG) 32–3
amphibious truck (DUKW)
        32, 44, 45, 63, 64, 67,
        78–9
Ancon 31
Anti-Air (AR) forces 31, 38
Anti-Submarine (AS)
        forces 31
Armoured Amphibious
        Vehicles see AAV
Artillery Lighters 16
assault craft 35

assaults 8
Attack Cargo Ship (AKA) 25
Aurelia 23
Autonomous Underwater
        Vehicle (AUV) 35
Avenger 87

B
Barbey, Rear-Admiral Daniel E.
        53, 68, 70
Beach, Armoured Recovery
        Vehicle (BARV) 36
beach obstructions 34
beachheads 36–7, 47
beaching vessels 39
Betio 54–5
Biak 69
Birmingham 71
Bismarck Sea 75
Blue Ridge 30
bombardment 7, 20, 34, 46,
        49, 57, 64, 67, 80, 89
Bombardment Liaison
        Officers 46
bombing 57, 64
Bonin Islands 72
Bougainville 49, 51
Buffalos see Landing Vehicle,
        Tracked
Bulolo 26
Bunker Hill 77

C
Cabilido 84
Cadiz (1587) 8–9
Canberra 86
Carolina Islands 66
Carter Hall 90
cartographers 28
Casablanca 25
Childers, Erskine 14
Chongjin (1950) 28
Churchill, Winston 10, 40
Clark, General Mark W.
        46, 47
close formations 32
Coastwatchers 50
command and control 30–1
command ships 30, 31,
        57, 73
Commanders, Amphibious
        Task Force (CATF) 30, 31

Commanders, Land Forces
        (CLF) 30, 31
commandos 40–1, 64,
        65, 86
Conqueror 87, 88
Coral Sea, Battle of the 49
Corunna/Vigo (1809) 9
Cunningham, Admiral
        Andrew B. 24, 45
current trends 90–1

D
D-Day see Operation
        "Overlord"
Daffodil 13
demonstrations 8, 9
desants 9
Dieppe (1942) 9, 20–1, 34,
        58, 64
Diligence 33
Doyen 54
DUKW amphibious trucks
        32, 44, 45, 63, 64, 67,
        78–9
Dulag 70
Dunkirk (1940) 9

E
Eisenhower, General Dwight D.
        24, 45
Eldorado 73
Ellis, Lt Col. Earle H. 14, 16
Elsie Items 57
escort carriers (CVE) 46, 70
Essex 90
Eureka boats see Landing
        Craft, Vehicle, Personnel
exercise "Cobra Gold" 9

F
Falklands (1982) 8, 33, 86–9
Far East Campaign (Japan)
        (1941–42) 18–19
feints 8, 9
Fleet Air Arm 88
Fleet Landing Exercises 17
Fleet Marine Force (FMF) 17
Fletcher, Vice-Admiral Frank
        22, 23, 31
Formosa (Taiwan) (1942) 19
Fort Austin 33
Fritz-X glider bombs 47

G
Gallipoli (1914) 7, 8, 9,
        10–11, 17, 30
Galveston 84
General Belgrano 88
Gibraltar (1704) 6
Gilbert Islands 54–5, 56
gliders 43
Guadalcanal 22–3, 37, 49,
        50, 54
Guam 16, 49, 66, 67
Guided Missile Cruiser (CG)
        91
Gulf War 90–1

H
Haig, Field Marshal Douglas 12
Halsey, Vice-Admiral William F.
        50, 70, 71
Hamilton, General Sir Ian 11
headquarters ships
        see command ships
helicopters 33, 82, 83
    Bell–Boeing Osprey 35
    Boeing Chinook 86
        Westland Sea King 88
        Westland Wessex 89
        Westland Whirlwind 83
Henderson 17
Hermes 89
Hewitt, Rear-Admiral Henry
        Kent 25, 44
Higgins, Andrew Jackson 17
Higgins Boats see Landing
        Craft, Vehicle, Personnel
Hollandia 88, 89
hospital ships 33
hovercraft 7, 32, 33, 37, 91
Hydra 33

I
Inca 76
Inchon class 80–1, 90
Inphigenia 13
inter-service relations 30
Intrepid 13
Invincible 89
Iris 13
Iwo Jima 49, 72–5

J
Jean Bart 26

K

kamikaze attacks 35, 74, 75, 76
Kerama Retto 76
Kesselring, Field Marshal Albert 46, 47
Keyes, Vice-Admiral Sir Roger 12, 13
King, Admiral Ernest J. 24, 94
Kinkaid, Vice-Admiral Thomas 70, 71
Kirk, Rear-Admiral Alan G. 60, 62
Kitchener, Field Marshal Horatio 11
Krebs 41
Krueger, Lieutenant General Walter 70
Kuribayashi, Lieutenant General Tadamichi 72, 74
Kurita, Vice-Admiral Takeo 71
Kwajalein 49, 56–7

L

Lae 49, 52–3, 68, 69
landing craft 14, 15, 16, 18
Landing Craft, Air Cushion (LCAC) 7, 32, 33, 37, 91
Landing Craft, Amphibious (LCA) 20, 25, 26, 38, 41, 61
Landing Craft, Control (LCC) 67
Landing Craft, FlaK (LCF) 64
Landing Craft, Gun (LCG) 64–5
Landing Craft, Infantry (LCI) 45, 57, 59, 61, 65, 67, 77
Landing Craft, Mechanized (LCM) 23, 25, 39, 41, 42, 52, 54, 87
Landing Craft, Personnel (LCP) 22
Landing Craft, Support (LCS) 73
Landing Craft, Tank (LCT) 9, 21, 32, 44, 50, 60, 61, 63, 64
Landing Craft, Utility (LCU) 32
Landing Craft, Vehicle, Personnel (LCVP) 15, 22, 32, 54, 57, 61, 67, 80

Landing Operations Doctrine (LOD) 17
Landing Ship, Dock (LSD) 9, 32, 57, 61, 67, 82, 84, 91
Landing Ship, Helicopter, Assault (LHA) 91
Landing Ship, Infantry (LSI) 32, 41
Landing Ship, Medium (LSM) 72, 74, 76
Landing Ship, Personnel, Dock (LPD) 91
Landing Ship, Personnel, Helicopter (LPH) 91
Landing Ship, Tank (LST) 25, 32, 38, 39, 44, 47, 50, 52, 53, 56, 57, 60, 61, 69, 80, 81, 91
Landing Vehicle, Tracked (LVT) 48, 54, 55, 56, 57, 64, 65, 66, 67, 73, 75, 77, 80, 83
Landing Vehicle, Tracked, Personnel (LVTP) 91
Leahy, Admiral William 29
leapfrog landings (desants) 9
Leonard Wood 42
Leyte 37, 49, 70–1
Lofoten Islands (1941) 40
logistics 38–9
Luzon 49

M

MacArthur, General Douglas 29, 52, 66, 68, 69, 70, 71, 80, 81
McCawley 51
Madang 69
Makin 49, 54–5
Mandates 16
Mariana Islands 57, 66–7
Marine Expeditionary Force (MEF) 91
Marine Expeditionary Units (MEU) 91
Marshall, General George C. 24

Marshall Islands 54, 56–7, 66
Massachusetts 26
merchant ship availability 38–9, 86, 87
Middle East 90–1
Midway, Battle of 22, 49
Mikawa, Vice-Admiral Gunichi 23
Military Sealift Command (MSC) 39
Mindoro 49
mines 34, 61–2
Minorca (1708) 8
Missouri 28, 29
Mitscher, Vice-Admiral Marc 76
Montgomery, General Bernard 45, 47
Motor Launch (ML) 12, 13, 20
Motor Torpedo Boat (MTB) 45
Mount Suribachi *see* Iwo Jima
Mulberry harbour 47, 58, 63
Munda 50, 51

N

naval aircraft *see* aircraft
Naval Gunfire Support (NGS) 7, 20, 34, *see also* bombardment
Nevada 49
New Britain 49
New Georgia 50–1
New Guinea 49, 52–3, 68–9
Nimitz, Admiral Chester 29, 52, 54, 56, 57, 68, 70, 71
Noemfoor 69
Norman Conquest (1066) 8

Normandy (1944) 8, 34, 35, 36–7, 59–63
North Africa *see* Operation "Torch"

O

Oak Hill 96
Ocean 82, 83, 91
Okinawa 49, 76–7
Olmeda 33
Operations
"Avalanche" 46–7
"Chromite" 80–1
"Claymore" 40
"Corporate" 86–89
"Desert Shield" 30
"Desert Storm" 30
"Detachment" 48, 72–5
"Flintlock" 56–7
"Forager" 66–7
"Galvanic" 54–5
"Husky" 42–5
"Iceberg" 76–7
"Infatuate II" 64–5
"Jubilee" 20–1
"Menace" 135
"Musketeer" 82–3
"Overlord" 59–63
"Postern" 52–3
"Reckless" 69
"Shoestring" 22
"Starlite" 84–5
"Toenails" 50–1
"Torch" 22, 24–7, 31
"Watchtower" 22–3, 31
"ZO" 12–13
Ostend (1918) 8, 12–13
Over-The-Horizon (OTH) operations 7, 33
Oyster pressure mine 61
Ozawa, Vice-Admiral Jisaburo 67

RIGHT: **US Rangers on board a British-manned LCA waiting to be taken to a transport ship in preparation for the assault on Pointe du Hoc (Normandy) on June 6, 1944.**

P

Pacific campaign (World
    War II) 8, 14–17, 48–9
Patton, Major General George
    31, 44, 45
Pearl Harbor 30
Pearl Harbor attack (1941) 18
Perdita 10
Philadelphia 6, 46
Philippine Sea, Battle
    of the 67
Philippines 16, 19, 48
Plan Orange 14–17, 38
Plassey 6
Plymouth 87
Pocono 30
pre-landing operations
    34–5
President Hayes 23
Prince Baudouin 61
Princess Beatrix 40
Princeton 71

Q

Quincy 23

R

raids 8, 9
Ramsey, Admiral Sir Bertram
    24, 60
Ranger 26
Rendova 50–1
Replenishment At Sea
    (RAS) 39
Rhino ferries 36, 39
River Clyde 11
Robert Rowan 43

Roi-Namur 56–7
Roll-on, Roll-off (Ro-Ro)
    transports 39
Rommel, Field Marshal
    Erwin 58
Roosevelt 90
Roosevelt, President
    Franklin D. 24, 29
Rundstedt, Field Marshal
    Gerd von 58

S

St. Nazaire (1942) 8, 9
Saipan 49, 66–7
Salamaua 49, 52–3, 68
Salerno (1943) 46–7, 67
Salvo Island, Battle of 23
Samar 71
sampans 84
San Antonio 90
San Bernadino Strait 71
Sanders, Marshal General
    Liman von 10
Sansapor 69
Saratoga 75
satellite surveillance 34
Sealines of Communication
    (SLOC) 88
Ships Taken Up From Trade
    (STUFT) 87
Sicily (1943) 42–5, 46
Smith, Major General
    Holland M. 55, 66
Solomon Islands 22–3,
    49, 50
Somali 41
South African (Boer) War 6
Special Landing Force
    (SLF) 84
Sprague, Rear-Admiral
    Thomas 70, 71
Spruance, Vice-Admiral
    Raymond 54, 57, 67

submarines 33, 34
Suce Action Groups (SAG)
    31
Suez 82–3, 90
Sumter 57, 66
supply ships 33
Support Squadron
    64–5
Surf Boats 103
Surigao Strait 71
Suvla *see* Gallipoli
Swift Boat *see* Patrol
    Craft, Fast
Swimmer Delivery Vehicle
    (SWD) 35

T

tactical nuclear weapons 35
Tanahmera Bay 68, 69
tank lighters 96
tanks
    amphibious 17, 34, 60,
        62–3
    Japanese 19
    M3 light 23
    M4 Sherman 47, 60, 67,
        68, 77
    Matilda 69
    Sherman Crab 65
Tarawa 49, 54–5, 56
Tedder, Air Chief Marshal
    Arthur 45
Tennessee 7
Tentative Landing Operations
    Manual (TLOM) 17
Termoli (1943) 9
Theseus 82, 83
Thetis 13
Tinian 66
Tokyo Express 51
Toulon (1793) 9
Trincomalee (1795) 8
Tsushima (1905) 15
Tulagi 22, 23, 49
Turner, Rear-Admiral
    Richmond K. 22, 50,
        51, 73

U

Uganda 33
Underwater Demolition
    Teams (UDT) 34
Unruffled 42
US Marine Corps
    (USMC) 14–17, 35,
        51, 54, 67, 68, 84

V

Vian, Rear-Admiral Sir
    Philip 60
Vietnam 84–5
Vindictive 12, 13

W

Walcheren 64–5
Wewak 69
Wilkinson, Vice-Admiral
    Eugene 70
Willis, Vice-Admiral Sir
    Algernon 45
withdrawal 8, 9
Wolmi 80
Wright 31

Y

Yorktown 6

Z

Zeebrugge (1918) 8, 9,
    12–13

ACKNOWLEDGEMENTS

Picture research for this book
was carried out by Jasper
Spencer-Smith, who has selected
images from the following
sources: JSS Collection,
Cody Images, Getty Images,
Imperial War Museum,
US Navy Archive and Topfoto.
(l=left, r=right, t=top,
b=bottom, m=middle):

Cody Images: 6b, 7bl, 7br, 10t,
11b, 14–15, 16–17, 18b, 22–3,
24, 25t, 27b, 28m, 28b, 29m,
29b, 34t, 34mr, 34br, 35br, 36b,
37b, 39, 42t, 45t, 46t, 46bl, 51b,
52, 54tl, 54br, 55t, 56t, 59,
62–3b, 64mr, 65t, 66b, 70, 72b,
73b, 75, 78b, 79b, 82mr, 83tl,
83ml, 86tr, 86mr, 88.
Topfoto: 19t, 20tl, 21b, 74tl, 84b.
US Navy (public domain): 4l,
5l, 35t, 36t, 38t, 38bl, 47t, 47b,
48–9, 60b, 71br, 73t, 76tl.
**UK MoD Crown Copyright
2010:** 6t, 92b.
Every effort has been made
to acknowledge photographs
correctly, however we apologize
for any unintentional omissions,
which will be corrected in
future editions.

BELOW: **A Type 072-II (Yuting II)
during an exercise for the
amphibious forces of the People's
Liberation Army in China.**